FATHER AND SON
FIGHTING FOR THE SAME CAUSE

Norma Iris Pagan Morales

ISBN 978-1-959895-96-1 (paperback)
ISBN 978-1-959895-95-4 (ebook)

Printed in the United States of America

WESTPOINT
PRINT AND MEDIA

OVERVIEW

The Korean War was fought between North Korea and South Korea from 1950 to 1953. The war began on 25 June 1950 when North Korea invaded South Korea following clashes along the border and rebellions in South Korea.

North Korea was supported by China and the Soviet Union while South Korea was supported by the United States and allied countries. The fighting ended with an armistice on 27 July 1953.

In 1910, Imperial Japan annexed Korea, where it ruled for 35 years until its surrender at the end of World War II on 15 August 1945. The United States and the Soviet Union divided Korea along the 38th parallel into two zones of occupation.

The Soviets administered the northern zone, and the Americans administered the southern zone. In 1948, because of Cold War tensions, the occupation zones became two sovereign states.

A communist state, the Democratic People's Republic of Korea, was established in the north under the totalitarian rule of Kim Il Sung, while a capitalist state, the Republic of Korea, was established in the south under the autocratic leadership of Syngman Rhee. Both governments claimed to be the sole legitimate government of all of Korea, and neither accepted the border as permanent.

Since Puerto Rico is a commonwealth of the United State, every Boricua had to be prepared to fight any war that the United is involved.

This is the story of my Grandfather Julio Pagan and my father Juan J. Pagan. Together they went to Korea and fought for our country.

CONTENTS

Overview.. iii

Chapter 1.   Father and Son fighting for the Same Cause 1

Chapter 2.   Getting Deployed 3

Chapter 3.   Waiting for The Worst..5

Chapter 4.   Sgt. Juan J. Pagan Rodriguez in Korea 8

Chapter 5.   Korean War 12

Chapter 6.   Korea divided (1945–1949)...16

Chapter 7.   Chinese Civil War (1945–1949) 19

Chapter 8.   Communist Insurgency in South Korea 1948–1950......21

Chapter 9.   Prelude to War 1950..24

Chapter 10. Comparison of Forces..27

Chapter 11. Course of the War..29

Chapter 12. Factors in U.S. intervention...31

Chapter 13. United States' Response July–August 1950 34

Chapter 14. The Drive South and Pusan July–September 1950 36

Chapter 15. Battle of Incheon (September 1950) 39

Chapter 16. Breakout from the Pusan Perimeter...............................41

Chapter 17. UN forces Invade North Korea (September–
             October 1950)...43

Chapter 18. China intervenes (October–December 1950) 46

Chapter 19. Soldiers from the US 2nd Infantry Division in
             action near the Ch'ongch'on River 20 November 1950 ...50

Chapter 20. Fighting around the 38th Parallel January–June 1951....53

Chapter 21. British UN troops advance alongside a
Centurion tank, March 1951...58

Chapter 22. Stalemate July 1951 – July 1953..............................61

Chapter 23. U.S. M46 Patton tanks, painted with tiger
heads thought to demoralize Chinese forces...................63

Chapter 24. New Zealand artillery crew in action, 1952 65

Chapter 25. Armistice July 1953 – November 1954.........................67

Chapter 26. Division of Korea 1954–present 70

Chapter 27. Military 74

Chapter 28. A soldier of the Dutch Detachment of the UN
forces in North Korea prepares to return sniper
fire, 1952...78

Chapter 29. Naval warfare...81

Chapter 30. Bombing of North Korea...86

Chapter 31. A USAF Douglas B-26B Invader of the 452nd
Bombardment Wing bombing a target in North
Korea, 29 May 1951..89

Chapter 32. U.S. threat of Atomic Warfare 91

Chapter 33. War Crimes 96

Chapter 34. Prisoners of War (POWs)..99

Chapter 35. Two men without shirts on sit surrounded by soldiers ...102

Chapter 36. Recreation 105

Chapter 37. Aftermath 106

Chapter 38. The Korean Peninsula at night, shown in a
2012 composite photograph from NASA 108

Chapter 39. North Koreans touring the Museum of
American War Atrocities in 2009.................................110

Chapter 40. The Forgotten Heroes of a Forgotten War 112

Chapter 41. Puerto Ricans Missing in action in the Korean War 120

Chapter 42. Military History of Puerto Rico................................127

Chapter 43. European powers fight over Puerto Rico 131

Chapter 44. American Revolutionary War................................136

Chapter 45. "La Rogativa" folklore.......................................139

Chapter 46. Revolt against Spain...144

Chapter 47. María de las Mercedes Barbudo 147

Chapter 48. Puerto Rico 149

Chapter 49. Ramón Emeterio Betances................................151

Chapter 50. Intentona de Yauco...153

Chapter 51. Cuba 154

Chapter 52. Puerto Rico National Guard...............................161

Chapter 53. Spanish Civil War 1936–1939 167

Chapter 54. "The Fighting Medinas" 170

Chapter 55. Commanders..174

Chapter 56. Revolt against the United States............................179

Chapter 57. Cold War 1947–1991 181

Chapter 58. Mass court-martial...186

Chapter 59. 21st century campaigns 191

Chapter 60. 65th Infantry Regiment United States 194

Chapter 61. Battles of Outpost Kelly and Jackson Heights............203

Chapter 62. Awards in the Korean War 206

Chapter 63. Legacy 212

Chapter 64. Congressional Gold Medal 215

Chapter 65. The Korean War the first time Puerto Rican
troops were thrown in.....................................217

References 223

About the Author...227

CHAPTER 1

Father and Son fighting for the Same Cause

The following four stories are about my father and grandfather. They were American Soldiers serving our nation with pride.

In the early spring, in 1950, The Puerto Rico Army National Guard was training every soldier harder than ever. Everyone knew that soon the National Guard would be mobilized.

My mother and grandmother were sad during those days because they knew that every member in my family will be deployed to Korea.

Since my mother was pregnant with her second child, she was too big to work around the house. My grandmother, Guadalupe, let her rest because my mother was due soon. This time, both my grandmother Guadalupe and my great-grandmother had a bad feeling about this child.

My mother was always too tired and didn't want to eat. I guess my mom was always sick because she didn't see my father often enough.

On October 20, 1950, my mother went into labor for more hours than expected. She gave birth to another baby girl, my sister, Adelin.

My grandmother Lupe and great grandma Dolores were happy because the baby was small, but healthy.

Digna, my mother, wanted to know if my father was around. My father and grandfather were doing drill at Losey Field base known today as Fort Allen in Juana Diaz, Puerto Rico.

Both my father and grandfather were happy because the new baby was doing well. They wanted to go home, but all passes were denied.

Juan Jose Pagan Rodriguez, my dad, got very angry when he was told that he couldn't go to Ponce to see his family. He just wanted an hour pass to see his wife and daughter. The answer from the commander was no....

My father decided to jump the fence...

So, when his unit went on break, he started walking very fast. There were sugar cane fields before reaching the main road.

As soon as he reached the street, a car stopped and to my father's surprise, it was his commander. The commander looked at him and told him to get in the car. The young Sergeant was surprised because he was escorted to Ponce to see his family.

The commander told him to stay the rest of the evening, but to return to the base the following day. My mother was very happy to see him. Adelin and I were beside my mom when my dad arrived. The whole family had a wonderful night together.

During the months that followed, things were very rough. Lots of soldiers were sent to Korea. My grandfather and my father were waiting for their orders...

Our nation was facing one of the worst times of that era. Puerto Rico was waiting and willing to fight in Korea.

I am proud to say, that my father, CSM Juan José Pagán Rodriguez, of the Puerto Rico Army National Guard and my grandfather, Staff Sergeant Julio Pagán Torres, now both deceased, were among those brave soldiers fighting for our country in one of the bloodiest conflicts.

CHAPTER 2

Getting Deployed

To understand the commotion that was going on in the states and Puerto Rico, I will give you some facts of what our soldiers were facing during that period....

On July 1, 1950, the Army's 24th Infantry Division became the first U.S. troop to arrive in Korea. They were transferred from Japan passing through the Port of Pusan. The troops took up Positions in Taejon, about 75 miles south of Seoul.

A couple of days later July 19, 1950, the 25th Infantry arrived followed by the 1st Marine Brigade and the 2nd Infantry Division in late July.

Things were getting worse in Korea that on July 20, 1950, the casualties were increasing. More than 2,400 men or 30% were reported dead. Taejon fell under the arms of the enemy.

All Americans and the rest of world were alarmed. This meant that many were going to be called to serve their country. The Reserves and the National Guard will be mobilized.

Puerto Rico, a beautiful island located in the Caribbean, and a Commonwealth of the United States, was getting ready.

There was no cultural or language barrier holding those brave men. Those "Boricuas" were well trained. I am proud to say that three members of my family were in the National Army Guard.

They knew that it wouldn't be long for the guard to be called for active duty. All three were ready to serve their nation. They were Staff Sgt. Julio Pagan Torres, my grandfather, as signed to 65th Infantry 4 machine gun 30 calibers, Sgt. Juan J. Pagan Rodriguez, my father, assigned to 65th Infantry Heavy Mortal Co. and the youngest, my uncle, Cpl. Julio Pagan Rodríguez was assigned to Artillery.

By early September, the new troops were combat ready in hardened fighting units. The Puerto Rican National Guard was mobilized on September 10, 1950. Every "Boricua's" family was worried because their loved ones will leave to an unknown land. Many have never been abroad. Now, they must face a lot of hardships.

It didn't take long for a humble family in Ponce to hear the worst news ever. Their sons and husbands must report for duty. This was awful because all three soldiers were assigned to infantry or artillery. The women were devastated when they heard the news on the radio.

Staff Sgt. Julio Pagan Torres and Sgt. Juan J. Pagan Rodriguez received their orders. Their unit, the 65th Infantry was being mobilized.

Cpl. Julio Pagan Rodriguez wasn't called at this time.

The 65th Infantry was now divided. That meant father and son were separated. The 296 Infantry was sent to Tortuguero. They were divided into three groups, 2nd to Juana Diaz and the 3rd to Cayey.

CHAPTER 3

Waiting for The Worst

Everything was moving too fast. The Puerto Rico Army National Guard was giving orders left and right. There was no question asked. It didn't matter if there were one sole survivor in a family. Men were needed to go abroad and fight for their country.

Sgt. Juan J. Pagán Rodriguez was ready to fight; however, he had a young wife and two young children. Sgt. Julio Pagán Torres had also young ones. They had a big problem. There was also a possibility that Cpl. Julio Pagán Rodriguez might be call for active duty. They wanted to serve, but they had a family.

The following day, both father and son decided to speak to their commander. The commander found it quite unusual for members of the same family to be called for active duty.

He listened to their petition and wrote all the information given by my father and grandfather. He told Sgt. Juan Pagán Rodriguez that he was the one chosen to go to Korea and that Sgt. Julio Pagán Torres will stay in Puerto Rico.

What follows, will not only put you in tears, but will make you wonder...

In November 1950, Sgt. Juan J. Pagán Rodriguez said goodbye to his beloved wife and family. He was only 22 years old but was fully aware of his commitment. His father promised him that he would take care of the whole family. Sgt. Juan J. Pagán Rodriguez just said, "Bendición Papito" and got on the bus…

Many "Boricuas" were also leaving Puerto Rico. This was the saddest day for the whole island. Saying goodbye was very hard. The 65th Infantry had already sent soldiers to Korea. Those first infantry soldiers made history throughout the nation. They were known as "The Borinqueneers" The 65th Infantry Regiment started the assault on January 31, 1951.

No Word From Sgt Juan Pagan Rodriguez

The Pagán family was very confused during this crisis because right after Sgt. Juan J. Pagán Rodriguez left Puerto Rico, his father Staff Sgt. Julio Pagán received new orders. These orders stated that he was leaving for Korea in December 1950.

This was the worst Christmas gift that anyone could receive.

Now, Staff Sgt. Julio Pagán Torres was also leaving his family. He told his wife, Guadalupe, "No te apures, todo va a salir bien". He couldn't face his daughter in law, Digna. She was holding her youngest daughter Adelin.

Digna was too upset to say goodbye. Sgt. Juan J. Pagán Rodriguez left the island months before and no one knew his whereabouts. The so many visits to the Red Cross were made in vain.

Sgt. Julio Pagán Torres even went to his commander for an answer of his previous visit. The commander apologized for the awful mess and stated that he was sorry. He told Sgt. Pagán Torres those orders were revoked because they got to Washington too late. Communication was very slow in those days…….

Ill Feelings In The Front Lines

Sgt. Juan J. Pagán Rodriguez was already fighting in the front lines. He got to Korea in January 1951 and at this point he was uneasy. He had been away from his family for nearly two months and no news was received.

It was hard to get anything where he was stationed. His new acquired family was his buddies, fellow "BORICUAS". All of them were waiting for any kind of news from Puerto Rico.

In Ponce, Puerto Rico, things weren't that great. With the breadwinner gone, it wasn't easy to raise all those children. Guadalupe and Digna had to go to the Red Cross. They wanted to hear news from their husbands.

The Red Cross assured them that both father and son were fine. Food and emergency money were provided. Digna was worried because the youngest daughter was very ill. Adelin was a very fragile child and needed medical attention.

When the Red Cross saw the baby, they referred her to the best doctors. The child was well taken cared and recovered within months.

By the end of February, troops were sent to the front lines once again....

CHAPTER 4

Sgt. Juan J. Pagan Rodriguez in Korea

One morning, Sgt. Juan Jose Pagán Rodriguez was ordered to take a couple of guys to a designated area. Sgt. Pagán Rodriguez briefed his men and started walking.

It was a cold bitter day and a lot of snow on the ground. The young soldiers were still trying to get used to that weather. They were all melancholy because they missed their sunny and warm Puerto Rico.

Many had suffered from frost bites. It wasn't easy keeping those soldiers motivated. They haven't heard anything from their families in months.

As they were walking, Sgt. Pagán Rodriguez started telling funny stories. The soldiers felt at ease. They reached their destination point. There were many wounded and others were suffering from the cold. Sgt. Pagán Rodriguez and his Troop relieved those men.

The fire never seized. Sgt. Pagán Rodriguez has been on his post for nearly a week. He was hungry and so were his men. They needed clean uniforms and chow.

Sgt. Juan J. Pagán Rodriguez kept fighting even though he didn't receive any news from Puerto Rico.

Suddenly, he received a message. He was ordered to report to his Commander. The young sergeant was surprised, but at the same time was happy to take a shower and change his uniform. He was escorted to his superior and to his surprise, there was Staff Sergeant Julio Pagán Torres waiting for him.

Words couldn't describe the emotion that those two human beings were feeling. Tears of joy were rolling down their faces. Sgt. Pagán Rodriguez asked his father about the family. He was also puzzled and questioning his father's arrival...both....in Korea...

The Commander of the 65th Infantry told both father and son that they would have to wait for new orders. He also told them that they will leave for Puerto Rico soon....

Those orders never came. Sgt. Juan J. Pagán Rodriguez was once again separated from his father......

A couple of days have gone by....

Sgt. Juan J. Pagán Rodriguez and his men were going to another camp site.

They had a couple of jeeps with plenty of supply. Sgt. Pagán Rodriguez saw a troop right in front of him. They were going to the same unit.

At that point, Sgt. Juan Pagán Rodriguez got the surprise of his life. His father, Staff Sgt. Julio Pagán Torres was among those men! He called his father, and both rode on the same jeep.

Once they arrived at their designated area, their new commandant called them. This time he gave them written orders. That was the best news Sgt. Pagán Rodriguez had received. He was going home, and his father was going with him safe and sound.

Sgt. Pagán Rodriguez and Staff Sgt. Julio Pagán Torres didn't want to be part of the big reception that was waiting for them in Puerto Rico.....

They were the first father and son wearing the same uniform and fighting for the same cause, but they just wanted to see their family.

They went to Ponce without being noticed. A taxi driver was the only witness when they reached home. There were a few gathered in front of the house. None of them were aware that a taxi had stopped there.

The two sergeants got off the taxi very quietly and opened the gate. Digna and Guadalupe started running once they saw them. It was a great day for the Pagán Family.

The Korean War brought Puerto Rican soldiers their greatest visibility, highest awards, and most punishing losses. There were 43, 434 Puerto Ricans in this war and 39, 591 of them were volunteers.

The 65th Infantry was chosen to guard the nation. They received awards for their bravery. It was also the last group of soldiers to leave the combat zone. Some bullets were whizzing by them as they boarded the ship to evacuate.......

FOR THEIR SERVICE, I SALUTE OUR "BORICUA" Korean's Heroes. We will never forget them.

Staff Sergeant Julio Pagán Torres and Sergeant Juan J. Pagán Rodríguez were the first father and son to serve the nation. They were in combat together and together returned to Ponce, Puerto Rico.

CSM Juan J. Pagán Rodriguez, my father, was very proud of being a soldier during the Korean Conflict. He told me how each soldier was being verbally abuse. Also, let me remain you, that when the first group went to Korea, they were not given the proper winter uniform. They still fought without any complaint....

CSM JUAN J. PAGAN RODRIGUEZ
This poem is dedicated to my dad
Born 01/29/1929 Died 03/28/2020
MY HERO
In choosing of becoming an NCO...
You accepted many responsibilities
In choosing of becoming a father...
You accepted many responsibilities
You are a role model, a trainer, and a loving father...
My hero...
As I sit here, thoughts of yesteryears come to mind...
You my father and a soldier...

FATHER AND SON FIGHTING FOR THE SAME CAUSE

Dealing with your family
Dealing with your troop…
Both tasks closely related and hard
An Army Non-Commissioned Officer and a father
Of four…
Your wisdom of many years made you a great leader…
Your wisdom of many years made you the father you are…
I salute you dear father…
I salute you for all the years
You devoted to us and to our nation

CHAPTER 5

Korean War

After many attempts of negotiations on unification, North Korean military, Korean People's Army, KPA, forces crossed the border and drove into South Korea on 25 June 1950.

The United Nations Security Council denounced North Korea's actions as an invasion and authorized the formation of the United Nations Command and the dispatch of forces to Korea to repel it.

The Soviet Union was boycotting the UN for recognizing Taiwan, Republic of China, as China. The People's Republic of China was not recognized by the UN, so neither could support their ally North Korea at the Security Council meeting.

Twenty-one countries of the United Nations eventually contributed to the UN force, with the United States providing around 90% of the military personnel.

After the first two months of war, the South Korean Army, ROKA, and hastily dispatched American forces were on the point of defeat, retreating to a small area behind a defensive line known as the Pusan Perimeter.

In September 1950, a risky amphibious UN counteroffensive was launched at Incheon, cutting off KPA troops and supply lines in South Korea. Those who escaped envelopment and capture were forced back north.

UN forces invaded North Korea in October 1950 and moved rapidly towards the Yalu River, the border with China, but on 19 October 1950, Chinese forces of the People's Volunteer Army, PVA, crossed the Yalu and entered the war.

The UN retreated from North Korea after the First Phase Offensive and the Second Phase Offensive. Chinese forces were in South Korea by late December.

In these and subsequent battles, Seoul was captured four times, and communist forces were pushed back to positions around the 38th parallel, close to where the war had started.

After this, the front stabilized, and the last two years were a war of attrition. The war in the air, however, was never a stalemate. North Korea was subject to a massive U.S. bombing campaign.

Jet-powered fighters confronted each other in air-to-air combat for the first time in history, and Soviet pilots covertly flew in defense of their communist allies.

The fighting ended on 27 July 1953 when the Korean Armistice Agreement was signed. The agreement created the Korean Demilitarized Zone, DMZ, to separate North and South Korea and allowed the return of prisoners.

However, no peace treaty was ever signed, and the two Koreas are technically still at war, engaged in a frozen conflict.

In April 2018, the leaders of North and South Korea met at the DMZ and agreed to work toward a treaty to end the Korean War formally.

The Korean War was among the most destructive conflicts of the modern era, with approximately 3 million war fatalities and a larger proportional civilian death toll than World War II or the Vietnam War. It incurred the destruction of virtually all of Korea's major cities, thousands of massacres by both sides, including the mass killing of tens of thousands of suspected communists by the South Korean government. There was torture and starvation of many prisoners of war by the North Koreans.

North Korea became among the most heavily bombed countries in history. 1.5 million North Koreans are estimated to have fled North Korea over the course of the war.

In the U.S., the war was initially described by President Harry S. Truman as a "police action", as the United States never formally declared war on its opponents and the operation was conducted under the auspices of the United Nations.

It has been sometimes referred to in the English-speaking world as "The Forgotten War" or "The Unknown War" because of the lack of public attention it received both during and after the war, relative to the global scale of World War II, which preceded it, and the subsequent torment of the Vietnam War, which succeeded it.

Let me give you some background information about this conflict....

Imperial Japanese rule 1910–1945

Imperial Japan severely diminished the influence of China over Korea in the First Sino-Japanese War, 1894–95, ushering in the short-lived Korean Empire.

A decade later, after defeating Imperial Russia in the Russo-Japanese War 1904–05, Japan made the Korean Empire its protectorate with the Eulsa Treaty in 1905, then annexed it with the Japan–Korea Annexation Treaty in 1910.

After that, the Korean Empire fell, and Korea was directly ruled by Japan from 1910 to 1945. That was when many Korean nationalists fled the country.

The Provisional Government of the Republic of Korea was founded in 1919 in Nationalist China. It failed to achieve international recognition, failed to unite the various nationalist groups, and had a fractious relationship with its U.S.-based founding president, Syngman Rhee.

From 1919 to 1925 and beyond, Korean communists led internal and external warfare against the Japanese.

In China, the nationalist National Revolutionary Army, and the communist People's Liberation Army (PLA) helped organize Korean refugees against the Japanese military, which had also occupied parts of China.

The Nationalist-backed Koreans, led by Yi Pom-Sok, fought in the Burma Campaign, December 1941 – August 1945. The communists, led among others by Kim Il Sung, fought the Japanese in Korea and Manchuria.

At the Cairo Conference in November 1943, China, the United Kingdom, and the United States all decided that "in due course Korea shall become free and independent".

CHAPTER 6

Korea divided (1945–1949)

At the Tehran Conference in November 1943 and the Yalta Conference in February 1945, the Soviet Union promised to join its allies in the Pacific War within three months of the victory in Europe.

Germany officially surrendered on 8 May 1945, and the USSR declared war on Japan and invaded Manchuria on 8 August 1945, three months later. This was three days after the atomic bombing of Hiroshima. By 10 August, the Red Army had begun to occupy the north of Korea.

On the night of 10 August in Washington, U.S. Colonels Dean Rusk, and Charles H. Bonesteel III were assigned to divide Korea into Soviet and U.S. occupation zones and proposed the 38th Parallel as the dividing line.

This was incorporated into the U.S. General Order No. 1, which responded to the Japanese surrender on 15 August. Explaining the choice of the 38th Parallel, Rusk observed, "even though it was further north than could be realistically reached by U. S. forces in the event of Soviet disagreement.

We felt it important to include the capital of Korea in responsibility of American troops". He noted that he was "faced with the scarcity of U.S. forces immediately available and time and space factors which would make it difficult to reach very far north before Soviet troops could enter the area".

As Rusk's comments indicate, the U.S. doubted whether the Soviet government would agree to this. Soviet leader Joseph Stalin, however, maintained his wartime policy of co-operation, and on 16 August, the Red Army halted at the 38th Parallel for three weeks to await the arrival of U.S. forces in the south.

On 7 September 1945, General Douglas MacArthur issued Proclamation No. 1 to the people of Korea, announcing U.S. military control over Korea south of the 38th parallel and establishing English as the official language during military control.

On 8 September 1945, U.S. Lieutenant General John R. Hodge arrived in Incheon to accept the Japanese surrender south of the 38th Parallel. Appointed as military governor, Hodge directly controlled South Korea as head of the United States Army Military Government in Korea (USAMGIK 1945–48).

In December 1945, Korea was administered by a U.S.–Soviet Union Joint Commission, as agreed at the Moscow Conference, with the aim of granting independence after a five-year trusteeship.

The idea was not popular among Koreans and riots broke out. To contain them, the USAMGIK banned strikes on 8 December 1945 and outlawed the PRK Revolutionary Government and the PRK People's Committees on 12 December 1945.

Following further large-scale civilian unrest, the USAMGIK declared martial law.

Mentioning the inability of the Joint Commission to make progress, the U.S. government decided to hold an election under United Nations auspices with the aim of creating an independent Korea.

The Soviet authorities and the Korean Communists refused to co-operate on the grounds that it would not be fair, and many South Korean politicians boycotted it.

A general election was held in the South on 10 May 1948. North Korea held parliamentary elections three months later, on 25 August.

The resultant South Korean government promulgated a national political constitution on 17 July 1948, and elected Syngman Rhee as

President on 20 July 1948. This election is generally considered to have been late regulated by the Rhee regime.

The Republic of Korea, South Korea, was established on 15 August 1948. In the Soviet Korean Zone of Occupation, the Soviet Union agreed to the establishment of a communist government led by Kim Il Sun.

The Soviet Union withdrew its forces from Korea in 1948, and U.S. troops withdrew in 1949.

CHAPTER 7

Chinese Civil War (1945–1949)

Chinese Civil War and Chinese Communist Revolution

With the end of the war with Japan, the Chinese Civil War resumed in earnest between the Communists and the Nationalist-led government.

While the Communists were struggling for supremacy in Manchuria, they were supported by the North Korean government with matériel and manpower.

According to Chinese sources, the North Koreans donated 2,000 railway cars worth of supplies while thousands of Koreans served in the Chinese PLA during the war.

North Korea also provided the Chinese Communists in Manchuria with a safe refuge for non-combatants and communications with the rest of China.

The North Korean contributions to the Chinese Communist victory were not forgotten after the creation of the People's Republic of China (PRC) in 1949.

As a token of gratitude, between 50,000 and 70,000 Korean veterans that served in the PLA were sent back along with their weapons, and they later played a significant role in the initial invasion of South

Korea. China promised to support the North Koreans in the event of a war against South Korea.

After the formation of the PRC, the PRC government named the Western nations, led by the U.S., as the biggest threat to its national security.

Creating this judgment on multiple factors, including the idea of a Chinese century of humiliation at the hands of Western powers beginning in the mid-19th century, U.S. support for the Nationalists during the Chinese Civil War, and the ideological struggles between revolutionaries and reactionaries, the PRC Chinese leadership believed that China would become a critical battleground in the U.S.' crusade against Communism.

As a countermeasure and to elevate China's standing among the worldwide Communist movements, the PRC leadership adopted a foreign policy that actively promoted Communist revolutions throughout territories on China's periphery.

CHAPTER 8

Communist Insurgency in South Korea 1948–1950

B y 1948, a large-scale, North Korea-backed insurgency had broken out in the southern half of the peninsula.

This was exacerbated by the ongoing undeclared border war between the Koreas, which saw division-level engagements and thousands of deaths on both sides.

The ROK in this time was almost entirely trained and focused on counterinsurgency, rather than conventional warfare. They were equipped and advised by a force of a few hundred American officers, who were largely successful in helping the ROKA to subdue guerrillas and hold its own against North Korean military, Korean People's Army, KPA, forces along the 38th parallel.

Approximately 8,000 South Korean soldiers and police died in the insurgent war and border clashes.

The first socialist uprising occurred without direct North Korean participation, though the guerrillas still professed support for the northern government.

Beginning in April 1948 on the isolated island of Jeju, the campaign saw mass arrests and repression by the South Korean government in the fight against the South Korean Labor Party, resulting in a total of 30,000 violent deaths, among them 14,373 civilians of whom ~2,000 were killed by rebels and ~12,000 by ROK security forces.

NORMA IRIS PAGAN MORALES

The Yeosu–Suncheon rebellion overlapped with it, as several thousand army defectors waving red flags massacred right-leaning families. This resulted in another brutal suppression by the government and between 2,976 and 3,392 deaths. By May 1949, both uprisings had been crushed.

Insurgency reignited in the spring of 1949 when attacks by guerrillas in the mountainous regions, buttressed by army defectors and North Korean agents, increased.

Insurgent activity peaked in late 1949 as the ROKA engaged so-called People's Guerrilla Units. Organized and armed by the North Korean government and backed up by 2,400 KPA commandos who had infiltrated through the border.

These guerrillas launched a large offensive in September aimed at undermining the South Korean government and preparing the country for the KPA's arrival in force.

This offensive failed, however, by this point, the guerrillas were firmly entrenched in the Taebaek-san region of the North Gyeongsang Province, around Taegu, as well as in the border areas of the Gangwon Province.

While the insurgency was ongoing, the ROKA and KPA engaged in multiple battalion-sized battles along the border, starting in May 1949.

Serious border clashes between South and North continued on 4 August 1949, when thousands of North Korean troops attacked South Korean troops occupying territory north of the 38th Parallel.

The 2nd and 18th ROK Infantry Regiments repulsed initial attacks in Kuksa-bong, above the 38th Parallel, and Ch'ungmu, and at the end of the clashes ROK troops were "completely routed". Border incidents decreased significantly by the start of 1950.

Meanwhile, counterinsurgency efforts in the South Korean interior intensified; persistent operations, paired with worsening weather conditions, eventually denied the guerrillas sanctuary, and wore away their fighting strength.

North Korea responded by sending more troops to link up with existing insurgents and build more partisan cadres; the number of North Korean infiltrators had reached 3,000 soldiers in 12 units by the start of 1950, but all these units were destroyed or scattered by the ROKA.

On 1 October 1949, the ROKA launched a three-pronged assault on the insurgents in South Cholla and Taegu. By March 1950, the ROKA claimed 5,621 guerrillas killed or captured and 1,066 small arms seized.

This operation crippled the insurgency. Soon after, the North Koreans made two final attempts to keep the uprising active, sending two battalion-sized units of infiltrators under the commands of Kim Sang-ho and Kim Moo-hyon.

The first battalion was reduced in annihilation to a single man over the course of several engagements by the ROKA 8th Division.

The second battalion was annihilated by a two-battalion hammer-and-anvil maneuver by units of the ROKA 6th Division, resulting in a loss toll of 584 KPA guerrillas, 480 killed, 104 captured, and 69 ROKA troops killed, plus 184 wounded. By spring of 1950, guerrilla activity had mostly subsided; the border, too, was calm.

CHAPTER 9

Prelude to War 1950

By 1949, South Korean and U.S. military actions had reduced the active number of indigenous communist guerrillas in the South from 5,000 to 1,000.

However, Kim Il Sung believed that widespread uprisings had weakened the South Korean military and that a North Korean invasion would be welcomed by much of the South Korean population. Kim began seeking Stalin's support for an invasion in March 1949, traveling to Moscow to attempt to persuade him.

Stalin initially did not think the time was right for a war in Korea. PLA forces were still embroiled in the Chinese Civil War, while U.S. forces remained stationed in South Korea.

By spring 1950, he believed that the strategic situation had changed: PLA forces under Mao Zedong had secured final victory in China, U.S. forces had withdrawn from Korea, and the Soviets had detonated their first nuclear bomb, breaking the U.S. atomic monopoly.

As the U.S. had not directly intervened to stop the communist victory in China, Stalin calculated that they would be even less willing to fight in Korea, which had much less strategic significance.

The Soviets had also cracked the codes used by the U.S. to communicate with their embassy in Moscow, and reading these dispatches convinced Stalin that Korea did not have the importance to the U.S. that would warrant a nuclear confrontation.

Stalin began a more aggressive strategy in Asia based on these developments, including promising economic and military aid to China through the Sino-Soviet Treaty of Friendship, Alliance, and Mutual Assistance.

In April 1950, Stalin gave Kim permission to attack the government in the South under the condition that Mao would agree to send reinforcements if needed.

For Kim, this was the fulfillment of his goal to unite Korea after its division by foreign powers. Stalin made it clear that Soviet forces would not openly engage in combat, to avoid a direct war with the U.S. Kim met with Mao in May 1950. Historical analyses regarding Mao's approval of Kim's plans differ.

Nikita Khrushchev's memoirs were long viewed as the most authoritative source, and Khrushchev wrote that Mao approved Kim's plans because Mao viewed the atter as one for the Korean people to decide for themselves.

There were29 recent scholarship, Zhao Suisheng, writing in 2022, contends that Mao did not approve of Kim's plans, opposing them over concerns that the U.S. would intervene, and that China could be dragged into the conflict.

By some accounts, Mao agreed to support the North Korean invasion despite these concerns, as China desperately needed the economic and military aid promised by the Soviets.

However, Mao sent more ethnic Korean PLA veterans to Korea and promised to move an army closer to the Korean border. Once Mao's commitment was secured, preparations for war accelerated.

Soviet generals with extensive combat experience from the Second World War were sent to North Korea as the Soviet Advisory Group. These generals completed the plans for the attack by May.

The original plans called for a skirmish to be initiated in the Ongjin Peninsula on the west coast of Korea. The North Koreans would then launch a counterattack that would capture Seoul and encircle and destroy the ROK.

The final stage would involve destroying South Korean government remnants and capturing the rest of South Korea, including the ports.

On 7 June 1950, Kim Il Sung called for a Korea-wide election on 5–8 August 1950 and a consultative conference in Haeju on 15–17 June 1950.

On 11 June, the North sent three diplomats to the South as a peace overture which Rhee rejected outright.

On 21 June, Kim Il Sung revised his war plan to involve a general attack across the 38th Parallel, rather than a limited operation in the Ongjin Peninsula. Kim was concerned that South Korean agents had learned about the plans and that South Korean forces were strengthening their defenses. Stalin agreed to this change of plan.

While these preparations were underway in the North, there were frequent clashes along the 38th Parallel, especially at Kaesong and Ongjin, many initiated by the South.

The ROK was being trained by the U.S. Korean Military Advisory Group (KMAG). On the eve of war, KMAG commander General William Lynn Roberts voiced utmost confidence in the ROK and boasted that any North Korean invasion would merely provide "target practice".

For his part, Syngman Rhee repeatedly expressed his desire to conquer the North, including when U.S. diplomat John Foster Dulles visited Korea on 18 June.

Although some South Korean and U.S. intelligence officers predicted an attack from the North, similar predictions had been made before and nothing had happened.

The Central Intelligence Agency noted the southward movement by the KPA but assessed this as a "defensive measure" and concluded an invasion was "unlikely".

On 23 June, UN observers inspected the border and did not detect that war was imminent.

CHAPTER 10

Comparison of Forces

Throughout 1949 and 1950, the Soviets continued arming North Korea. After the Communist victory in the Chinese Civil War, ethnic Korean units in the PLA were sent to North Korea.

Chinese involvement was extensive from the beginning, building on previous collaboration between the Chinese and Korean communists during the Chinese Civil War. In the fall of 1949, two PLA divisions composed mainly of Korean Chinese troops, the 164th and 166th, entered North Korea, followed by smaller units throughout the rest of 1949.

These troops brought with them not only their experience and training, but also their weapons and other equipment, changing little but their uniforms. The reinforcement of the KPA with PLA veterans continued into 1950, with the 156th Division and several other units of the former Fourth Field Army arriving, also with their equipment, in February; the PLA 156th Division was reorganized as the KPA 7th Division.

By mid-1950, between 50,000 and 70,000 former PLA troops had entered North Korea, forming a significant part of the KPA's strength on the eve of the war's beginning.

Several generals, such as Lee Kwon-mu, were PLA veterans born to ethnic Koreans in China. The combat veterans and equipment from China, the tanks, artillery, and aircraft supplied by the Soviets, and rigorous training increased North Korea's military superiority over the South, armed by the U.S. military with mostly small arms, but no heavy weaponry such as tanks.

While older histories of the conflict often referred to these ethnic Korean PLA veterans as being sent from northern Korea to fight in the Chinese Civil War before being sent back, recent Chinese archival sources studied by Kim Donggill indicate that this was not the case.

Somewhat, the soldiers were indigenous to China, part of China's longstanding ethnic Korean community, and were recruited to the PLA in the same way as any other Chinese citizen.

According to the first official census in 1949, the population of North Korea numbered 9,620,000, and by mid-1950, North Korean forces numbered between 150,000 and 200,000 troops, organized into 10 infantry divisions, one tank division, and one air force division, with 210 fighter planes and 280 tanks, who captured scheduled objectives and territory, among them Kaesong, Chuncheon, Uijeongbu and Ongjin.

Their forces included 274 T-34-85 tanks, 200 artillery pieces, 110 attack bombers, some 150 Yak fighter planes, and 35 reconnaissance aircraft. In addition to the invasion force, the North had 114 fighters, 78 bombers, 105 T-34-85 tanks, and some 30,000 soldiers stationed in reserve in North Korea.

Although each navy consisted of only several small warships, the North and South Korean navies fought in the war as seaborne artillery for their armies.

In contrast, the South Korean population was estimated at 20 million[145] and its army was unprepared and ill-equipped. As of 25 June 1950, the ROK had 98,000 soldiers, 65,000 combat, 33,000 support, no tanks.

They had been requested from the U.S. military, but requests were denied, and a 22-plane air force comprising 12 liaison-type and 10 AT-6 advanced-trainer airplanes. Large U.S. garrisons and air forces were in Japan, but only 200–300 U.S. troops were in Korea.

CHAPTER 11

Course of the War

Territory often changed hands early in the war, until the front stabilized.

Chinese and communist forces (Soviet Union)

North Korean forces

South Korean, U.S. and United Nations forces

Hundreds of thousands of South Koreans fled south in mid-1950 after the North Korean army invaded.

At dawn on Sunday, 25 June 1950, the KPA crossed the 38th Parallel behind artillery fire. The KPA justified its assault with the claim that ROK troops attacked first, and that the KPA were aiming to arrest and execute the "bandit traitor Syngman Rhee". Fighting began on the strategic Ongjin Peninsula in the west.

There were initial South Korean claims that the 17th Regiment captured the city of Haeju, and this sequence of events has led some scholars to argue that the South Koreans fired first.

Whoever fired the first shots in Ongjin, KPA forces attacked all along the 38th Parallel within an hour. The KPA had a combined arms force including tanks supported by heavy artillery.

The ROK had no tanks, anti-tank weapons or heavy artillery to stop such an attack. In addition, the South Koreans committed their forces in a piecemeal fashion, and these were routed in a few days.

On 27 June, Rhee evacuated from Seoul with some of the government. On 28 June, at 2 am, the ROK blew up the Hangang Bridge across the Han River to stop the KPA. The bridge was detonated while 4,000 refugees were crossing it and hundreds were killed.

Destroying the bridge also trapped many ROK units north of the Han River. Despite such desperate measures, Seoul fell that same day.

A few South Korean National Assemblymen remained in Seoul when it fell, and forty-eight subsequently pledged allegiance to the North.

On 28 June, Rhee ordered the massacre of suspected political opponents in his own country.

In five days, the ROK, which had 95,000 troops on 25 June, was down to less than 22,000 troops. In early July, when U.S. forces arrived, what was left of the ROK were placed under U.S. operational command of the United Nations Command.

CHAPTER 12

Factors in U.S. intervention

The Truman administration was unprepared for the invasion. Korea was not included in the strategic Asian Defense Perimeter outlined by United States Secretary of State Dean Acheson.

Truman himself was at his home in Independence, Missouri. Military strategists were more concerned with the security of Europe against the Soviet Union than East Asia.

At the same time, the administration was worried that a war in Korea could quickly escalate without American intervention. Said diplomat John Foster Dulles in a cable: "To sit by while Korea is overrun by unprovoked armed attack would start a disastrous chain of events leading most probably to world war."

While there was initial hesitance by some in the U.S. government to get involved in the war, considerations about Japan played a part in the ultimate decision to engage on behalf of South Korea. Especially after the fall of China to the Communists, U.S. experts on East Asia saw Japan as the critical counterweight to the Soviet Union and China in the region.

While there was no U.S. policy dealing with South Korea directly as a national interest, its proximity to Japan increased the importance of South Korea. Said Kim: "The recognition that the security of Japan required a non-hostile Korea led directly to President Truman's decision to intervene.

The essential point is that the American response to the North Korean attack stemmed from considerations of U.S. policy toward Japan."

Another major consideration was the possible Soviet reaction if the U.S. intervened. The Truman administration was fearful that a war in Korea was a diversionary assault that would escalate to a general war in Europe once the United States committed in Korea.

At the same time, "there was no suggestion from anyone that the United Nations or the United States could back away from the conflict".

Yugoslavia, a possible Soviet target because of the Tito-Stalin Split was vital to the defense of Italy and Greece, and the country was first on the list of the National Security Council's post-North Korea invasion list of "chief danger spots".

Truman believed if aggression went unchecked, a chain reaction would be initiated that would marginalize the UN and encourage Communist aggression elsewhere.

The UN Security Council approved the use of force to help the South Koreans, and the U.S. immediately began using air and naval forces that were in the area to that end.

The Truman administration still refrained from committing troops on the ground because some advisers believed the North Koreans could be stopped by air and naval power alone.

The Truman administration was still uncertain if the attack was a ploy by the Soviet Union or just a test of U.S. resolve. The decision to commit ground troops became viable when a communiqué was received on 27 June indicating the Soviet Union would not move against U.S. forces in Korea.

The Truman administration now believed it could intervene in Korea without undermining its commitments elsewhere.

United Nations Security Council Resolutions

Further information: List of United Nations Security Council resolutions concerning North Korea.

On 25 June 1950, the United Nations Security Council unanimously condemned the North Korean invasion of South Korea, with UN Security Council Resolution 82. The Soviet Union, a veto-wielding power, had boycotted the Council meetings since January 1950, protesting Taiwan's occupation of China's permanent seat in the UN Security Council. After debating the matter, the Security Council, on 27 June 1950, published Resolution 83 recommending member states provide military assistance to the Republic of Korea.

On 27 June, President Truman ordered U.S. air and sea forces to help South Korea. On 4 July, the Soviet Deputy Foreign Minister accused the U.S. of starting armed intervention on behalf of South Korea.

The Soviet Union challenged the legitimacy of the war for several reasons. The ROK intelligence upon which Resolution 83 was based came from U.S. Intelligence.

North Korea was not invited as a sitting temporary member of the UN, which violated UN Charter Article 32; and the fighting was beyond the UN Charter's scope, because the initial north–south border fighting was classed as a civil war.

Because the Soviet Union was boycotting the Security Council at the time, legal scholars posited that deciding upon an action of this type required the unanimous vote of all the five permanent members including the Soviet Union.

Within days of the invasion, masses of ROK soldiers—of dubious loyalty to the Syngman Rhee regime—were retreating southwards or defecting en masse to the northern side, the KPA.

CHAPTER 13

United States' Response July–August 1950

A group of soldiers readying a
large gun in some brush

M an of the Year, the American soldier on Time magazine cover,
1951

As soon as word of the attack was received, Acheson informed
President Truman that the North Koreans had invaded South Korea.

Truman and Acheson discussed a U.S. invasion response and agreed
that the U.S. was obligated to act, comparing the North Korean invasion
with Adolf Hitler's aggressions in the 1930s, with the conclusion being
that the mistake of appeasement must not be repeated.

Several U.S. industries were mobilized to supply materials, labor,
capital, production facilities, and other services necessary to support the
military objectives of the Korean War.

President Truman later explained that he believed fighting the
invasion was essential to the U.S. goal of the global containment of
communism as outlined in the National Security Council Report 68
(NSC 68), declassified in 1975.

Communism was acting in Korea, just as Hitler, Mussolini and
the Japanese had ten, fifteen, and twenty years earlier. I felt certain

that if South Korea was allowed to fall, Communist leaders would be emboldened to override nations closer to our own shores.

If the Communists were permitted to force their way into the Republic of Korea without opposition from the free world, no small nation would have the courage to resist threat and aggression by stronger Communist neighbors.

In August 1950, the President and the Secretary of State obtained the consent of Congress to appropriate $12 billion for military action in Korea, equivalent to $146 billion in 2022.

Because of the extensive defense cuts and the emphasis placed on building a nuclear bomber force, none of the services were able to make a robust response with conventional military strength.

General Omar Bradley, Chairman of the Joint Chiefs of Staff, was faced with reorganizing and deploying a U.S. military force that was a shadow of its World War II counterpart.

Acting on Secretary of State Acheson's recommendation, President Truman ordered Supreme Commander for the Allied Powers in Japan General Douglas MacArthur to transfer matériel to the South Korean military while giving air cover to the evacuation of U.S. nationals.

The President disagreed with advisers who recommended unilateral U.S. bombing of the North Korean forces and ordered the U.S. Seventh Fleet to protect the Republic of China (Taiwan), whose government asked to fight in Korea. The United States denied Taiwan's request for combat, lest it provoke a PRC retaliation.

Because the United States had sent the Seventh Fleet to "neutralize" the Taiwan Strait, Chinese premier Zhou Enlai criticized both the UN and U.S. initiatives as "armed aggression on Chinese territory".

CHAPTER 14

The Drive South and Pusan July–September 1950

Crew of an M-24 tank along the Nakong River front, August 1950

The Battle of Osan, the first significant U.S. engagement of the Korean War, involved the 540-soldier Task Force Smith, which was a small forward element of the 24th Infantry Division which had been flown in from Japan.

On 5 July 1950, Task Force Smith attacked the KPA at Osan but without weapons capable of destroying the KPA tanks. The KPA defeated the U.S. soldiers; the result was 180 American dead, wounded, or taken prisoner.

The KPA progressed southwards, pushing back U.S. forces at Pyongtaek, Chonan, and Chochiwon, forcing the 24th Division's retreat to Taejeon, which the KPA captured in the Battle of Taejon; the 24th Division suffered 3,602 dead and wounded and 2,962 captured, including its commander, Major General William F. Dean.

By August, the KPA steadily pushed back the ROK and the Eighth United States Army southwards. The impact of the Truman administration's defense budget cutbacks was now keenly felt, as U.S. troops fought a series of costly rearguard actions.

Facing a veteran and well-led KPA force, and lacking sufficient anti-tank weapons, artillery or armor, the Americans retreated and the KPA advanced down the Korean Peninsula.

During their advance, the KPA purged South Korea's intelligentsia by killing civil servants and intellectuals. On 20 August, General MacArthur warned North Korean leader Kim Il Sung that he would be held responsible for the KPA's atrocities.

By September, UN forces were hemmed into a small corner of southeast Korea, near Pusan. This 230-kilometre (140-mile) perimeter enclosed about 10% of Korea, in a line partially defined by the Nakdong River.

Although Kim's early successes led him to predict he would end the war by the end of August, Chinese leaders were more pessimistic. To counter a possible U.S. deployment, Zhou Enlai secured a Soviet commitment to have the Soviet Union support Chinese forces with air cover, and deployed 260,000 soldiers along the Korean border, under the command of Gao Gang.

Zhou commanded Chai Chengwen to conduct a topographical survey of Korea, and directed Lei Yingfu, Zhou's military advisor in Korea, to analyze the military situation in Korea. Lei concluded that MacArthur would most likely attempt a landing at Incheon.

After conferring with Mao that this would be MacArthur's most likely strategy, Zhou briefed Soviet and North Korean advisers of Lei's findings and issued orders to PLA commanders deployed on the Korean border to prepare for U.S. naval activity in the Korea Strait.

In the resulting Battle of Pusan Perimeter (August–September 1950), the UN forces withstood KPA attacks meant to capture the city at the Naktong Bulge, P'ohang-dong, and Taegu.

The United States Air Force (USAF) interrupted KPA logistics with 40 daily ground support sorties, which destroyed 32 bridges, halting most daytime road and rail traffic. KPA forces were forced to hide in tunnels by day and move only at night.

To deny military equipment and supplies to the KPA, the USAF destroyed logistics depots, petroleum refineries, and harbors, while the U.S. Navy air forces attacked transport hubs. Consequently, the overextended KPA could not be supplied throughout the south.

On 27 August, 67th Fighter Squadron aircraft mistakenly attacked facilities in Chinese territory and the Soviet Union called the UN Security Council's attention to China's complaint about the incident.

The U.S. proposed that a commission of India and Sweden determine what the U.S. should pay in compensation, but the Soviets vetoed the U.S. proposal.

Meanwhile, U.S. garrisons in Japan continually dispatched soldiers and military supplies to reinforce defenders in the Pusan Perimeter.

MacArthur went so far as to call for Japan's rearmament. Tank battalions deployed to Korea directly from the U.S. mainland from the port of San Francisco to the port of Pusan, the largest Korean port.

By late August, the Pusan Perimeter had some 500 medium tanks battle-ready.

In early September 1950, UN forces outnumbered the KPA 180,000 to 100,000 soldiers.

CHAPTER 15

Battle of Incheon (September 1950)

Combat in the streets of Seoul

Pershing tanks in downtown Seoul during the Second Battle of Seoul in September 1950. In the foreground, United Nations troops round up North Korean prisoners-of-war.

Against the rested and rearmed Pusan Perimeter defenders and their reinforcements, the KPA were undermanned and poorly supplied; unlike the UN forces, they lacked naval and air support.

To relieve the Pusan Perimeter, General MacArthur recommended an amphibious landing at Incheon, near Seoul and well over 160 km (100 mi) behind the KPA lines.

On 6 July, he ordered Major General Hobart R. Gay, commander of the U.S. 1st Cavalry Division, to plan the division's amphibious landing at Incheon; on 12–14 July, the 1st Cavalry Division embarked from Yokohama, Japan, to reinforce the 24th Infantry Division inside the Pusan Perimeter.

Soon after the war began, General MacArthur began planning a landing at Incheon, but the Pentagon opposed him.

When authorized, he activated a combined U.S. Army and Marine Corps, and ROK force. The U.S. X Corps, led by Major General Edward

Almond, consisted of 40,000 soldiers of the 1st Marine Division, the 7th Infantry Division and around 8,600 ROK soldiers.

By 15 September, the amphibious assault force faced few KPA defenders at Incheon: military intelligence, psychological warfare, guerrilla reconnaissance, and protracted bombardment facilitated a relatively light battle. However, the bombardment destroyed most of the city of Incheon.

CHAPTER 16

Breakout from the Pusan Perimeter

Pusan Perimeter offensive, UN September 1950
counteroffensive, and Second Battle of Seoul

On 16 September Eighth Army began its breakout from the Pusan Perimeter. Task Force Lynch, 3rd Battalion, 7th Cavalry Regiment, and two 70th Tank Battalion units, Charlie Company and the Intelligence, Reconnaissance Platoon, advanced through 171.2 km (106.4 mi) of KPA territory to join the 7th Infantry Division at Osan on 27 September.

X Corps rapidly defeated the KPA defenders around Seoul, thus threatening to trap the main KPA force in Southern Korea.

On 18 September, Stalin dispatched General H. M. Zakharov to North Korea to advise Kim Il Sung to halt his offensive around the Pusan perimeter and to redeploy his forces to defend Seoul. Chinese commanders were not briefed on North Korean troop numbers or operational plans.

As the overall commander of Chinese forces, Zhou Enlai suggested that the North Koreans should attempt to eliminate the UN forces at Incheon only if they had reserves of at least 100,000 men; otherwise, he advised the North Koreans to withdraw their forces north.

On 25 September, Seoul was recaptured by UN forces. U.S. air raids caused heavy damage to the KPA, destroying most of its tanks and much of its artillery. KPA troops in the south, instead of effectively withdrawing north, rapidly disintegrated, leaving Pyongyang vulnerable.

During the general retreat, only 25,000 to 30,000 KPA soldiers managed to reach the KPA lines.

On 27 September, Stalin convened an emergency session of the Politburo, in which he condemned the incompetence of the KPA command and held Soviet military advisers responsible for the defeat.

CHAPTER 17

UN forces Invade North Korea (September–October 1950)

UN offensive into North Korea

On 27 September, MacArthur received the top-secret National Security Council Memorandum 81/1 from Truman reminding him that operations north of the 38th Parallel were authorized only if "at the time of such operation there was no entry into North Korea by major Soviet or Chinese Communist forces, no announcements of intended entry, nor a threat to counter our operations militarily".

On 29 September, MacArthur restored the government of the Republic of Korea under Syngman Rhee.

On 30 September, U.S. Defense Secretary George Marshall sent an eyes-only message to MacArthur: "We want you to feel unhampered tactically and strategically to proceed north of the 38th parallel."

During October, the South Korean police executed people who were suspected to be sympathetic to North Korea, and similar massacres were carried out until early 1951.

The Joint Chiefs of Staff on 27 September sent to General MacArthur a comprehensive directive to govern his future actions: the directive stated that the primary goal was the destruction of the KPA, with unification of the Korean Peninsula under Rhee as a secondary objective "if possible"; the Joint Chiefs added that this objective was dependent on whether the Chinese and Soviets would intervene and was subject to changing conditions.

U.S. Air Force attacking railroads south of Wonsan on the eastern coast of North Korea

On 30 September, Zhou Enlai warned the U.S. that China was prepared to intervene in Korea if the U.S. crossed the 38th Parallel. Zhou attempted to advise KPA commanders on how to conduct a general withdrawal by using the same tactics that allowed Chinese communist forces to successfully escape Chiang Kai-shek's encirclement campaigns in the 1930s, but by some accounts, KPA commanders did not use these tactics effectively.

Historian Bruce Cummings argues, however, that the KPA's rapid withdrawal was strategic, with troops melting into the mountains from where they could launch guerrilla raids on the UN forces spread out on the coasts.

By 1 October 1950, the UN Command repelled the KPA northwards past the 38th Parallel; the ROK advanced after them, into North Korea.

MacArthur made a statement demanding the KPA's unconditional surrender. Six days later, on 7 October, with UN authorization, the UN Command forces followed the ROK forces northwards.

The X Corps landed at Wonsan, in southeastern North Korea, and Riwon, in northeastern North Korea, on 26 October, but these cities had already been captured by ROK forces.

The Eighth U.S. Army drove up western Korea and captured Pyongyang on 19 October 1950. The 187th Airborne Regimental Combat Team made their first of two combat jumps during the Korean War on 20 October 1950 at Sunchon and Sukchon.

The mission was to cut the road north going to China, preventing North Korean leaders from escaping from Pyongyang; and to rescue U.S.

prisoners of war. At month's end, UN forces held 135,000 KPA prisoners of war. As they neared the Sino-Korean border, the UN forces in the west were divided from those in the east by 80–161 km (50–100 mi) of mountainous terrain.

In addition to the 135,000 captured, the KPA had also suffered some 200,000 soldiers killed or wounded for a total of 335,000 casualties since the end of June 1950, and had lost 313 tanks, mostly T-34/85 models.

A mere 25,000 KPA regulars retreated across the 38th Parallel, as their military had entirely collapsed. The UN forces on the peninsula numbered 229,722 combat

Troops, including 125,126 Americans and 82,786 South Koreans, 119,559 rear area troops, and 36,667 U.S. Air Force personnel.

Taking advantage of the UN Command's strategic momentum against the communists, MacArthur believed it necessary to extend the Korean War into China to destroy depots supplying the North Korean war effort. Truman disagreed and ordered caution at the Sino-Korean border.

CHAPTER 18

China intervenes (October–December 1950)

Chinese forces cross the frozen Yalu River.

On 30 June 1950, five days after the outbreak of the war, Zhou Enlai, premier of the PRC and vice-chairman of the Central Military Committee of the CCP (CMCC), decided to send a group of Chinese military intelligence personnel to North Korea to establish better communications with Kim Il-Sung as well as to collect firsthand materials on the fighting.

One week later, on 7 July, Zhou and Mao chaired a conference discussing military preparations for the Korean Conflict. Another conference took place on 10 July.

Here, it was decided that the Thirteenth Army Corps under the Fourth Field Army of the People's Liberation Army (PLA), one of the best-trained and -equipped units in China, would be immediately transformed into the Northeastern Border Defense Army (NEBDA) to prepare for "an intervention in the Korean War if necessary".

On 13 July, the CMCC formally issued the order to establish the NEBDA, appointing Deng Hua, the commander of the Fifteenth Army Corps and one of the most talented commanders of the Chinese Civil War, to coordinate all preparation efforts.

On 20 August 1950, Premier Zhou Enlai informed the UN that "Korea is China's neighbor... The Chinese people cannot but be concerned about a solution of the Korean question". Thus, through neutral-country diplomats, China warned that in safeguarding Chinese national security, they would intervene against the UN Command in Korea.

President Truman interpreted the communication as "a bald attempt to blackmail the UN" and dismissed it.

Mao ordered that his troops should be ready for action by the end of August. Stalin, by contrast, was reluctant to escalate the war with a Chinese intervention.

On 1 October 1950, the day that UN troops crossed the 38th Parallel, the Soviet ambassador forwarded a telegram from Stalin to Mao and Zhou requesting that China send five to six divisions into Korea, and Kim Il Sung sent frantic appeals to Mao for Chinese military intervention.

At the same time, Stalin made it clear that Soviet forces themselves would not directly intervene.

Three commanders of the PVA during the Korean War. From left to right: Chen Geng 1952; Peng Dehuai, 1950–1952; and Deng Hua 1952–1953.

In a series of emergency meetings that lasted from 2 to 5 October, Chinese leaders debated whether to send Chinese troops into Korea. There was considerable resistance among many leaders, including senior military leaders, to confronting the U.S. in Korea.

Mao strongly supported intervention, and Zhou was one of the few Chinese leaders who firmly supported him. After Lin Biao politely refused Mao's offer to command Chinese forces in Korea, citing his upcoming medical treatment, Mao decided that Peng Dehuai would be the commander of the Chinese forces in Korea after Peng agreed to support Mao's position.

Mao then asked Peng to speak in favor of intervention to the rest of the Chinese leaders. After Peng made the case that if U.S. troops conquered Korea and reached the Yalu, they might cross it and invade China, the Politburo agreed to intervene in Korea.

On 4 August 1950, with a planned invasion of Taiwan aborted due to the heavy U.S. naval presence, Mao reported to the Politburo that he would intervene in Korea when the PLA's Taiwan invasion force was reorganized into the PLA Northeast Frontier Force.

On 8 October 1950, Mao redesignated the PLA Northeast Frontier Force as the People's Volunteer Army, PVA.

To enlist Stalin's support, Zhou and a Chinese delegation arrived in Moscow on 10 October, at which point they flew to Stalin's home on the Black Sea.

There, they conferred with the top Soviet leadership, which included Joseph Stalin as well as Vyacheslav Molotov, Lavrentiy Beria and Georgy Malenkov.

Stalin initially agreed to send military equipment and ammunition but warned Zhou that the Soviet Air Force would need two or three months to prepare any operations.

In a subsequent meeting, Stalin told Zhou that he would only provide China with equipment on a credit basis and that the Soviet Air Force would only operate over Chinese airspace, and only after an undisclosed period. Stalin did not agree to send either military equipment or air support until March 1951.

Mao did not find Soviet air support especially useful, as the fighting was going to take place on the south side of the Yalu. Soviet shipments of matériel, when they did arrive, were limited to small quantities of trucks, grenades, machine guns, and the like.

In a meeting on 13 October, the Politburo of the Chinese Communist Party decided that China would intervene even in the absence of Soviet air support, basing its decision on a belief that superior morale could defeat an enemy that had superior equipment.

Immediately on his return to Beijing on 18 October 1950, Zhou met with Mao Zedong, Peng Dehuai and Gao Gang, and the group ordered two hundred thousand PVA troops to enter North Korea, which they did on 19 October.

UN aerial reconnaissance had difficulty sighting PVA units in daytime because their march and bivouac discipline minimized aerial detection.

The PVA marched "dark-to-dark", 19:00–03:00, and aerial camouflage, concealing soldiers, pack animals, and equipment, was deployed by 05:30.

Meanwhile, daylight advance parties scouted for the next bivouac site. During daylight activity or marching, soldiers were to remain motionless if an aircraft appeared, until it flew away; PVA officers were under order to shoot security violators.

Such battlefield discipline allowed a three-division army to march the 460 km, 286 mi, from An-tung, Manchuria, to the combat zone in some 19 days. Another division night-marched a circuitous mountain route, averaging 29 km (18 mi) daily for 18 days.

Meanwhile, on 15 October 1950, President Truman and General MacArthur met at Wake Island. This meeting was much publicized because of the General's discourteous refusal to meet the President on the continental United States.

To President Truman, MacArthur speculated there was little risk of Chinese intervention in Korea, and that the PRC's opportunity for aiding the KPA had lapsed. He believed the PRC had some 300,000 soldiers in Manchuria and some 100,000–125,000 soldiers at the Yalu River.

Chinese tried to get down to Pyongyang, there would be the greatest slaughter" without air force protection.

CHAPTER 19

Soldiers from the US 2nd Infantry Division in action near the Ch'ongch'on River 20 November 1950

A column of the US 1st Marine Division move through Chinese lines during their breakout from the Chosin Reservoir.

After secretly crossing the Yalu River on 19 October, the PVA 13th Army Group launched the First Phase Offensive on 25 October, attacking the advancing UN forces near the Sino-Korean border.

This military decision made solely by China changed the attitude of the Soviet Union. Twelve days after PVA troops entered the war, Stalin allowed the Soviet Air Force to provide air cover and supported more aid to China.

After inflicting heavy losses on the ROK II Corps at the Battle of Onjong, the first confrontation between Chinese and U.S. military occurred on 1 November 1950.

Deep in North Korea, thousands of soldiers from the PVA 39th Army encircled and attacked the U.S. 8th Cavalry Regiment with three-prong assaults, from the north, northwest, and west and overran the defensive position flanks in the Battle of Unsan.

The surprise assault resulted in the UN forces retreating to the Ch'ongch'on River, while the PVA unexpectedly disappeared into mountain hideouts following victory. It is unclear why the Chinese did not press the attack and follow up their victory.

The UN Command, however, were unconvinced that the Chinese had openly intervened because of the sudden PVA withdrawal. On 24 November, the Home-by-Christmas Offensive was launched with the U.S. Eighth Army advancing in northwest Korea, while U.S. X Corps attacked along the Korean east coast. But the PVA were waiting in ambush with their Second Phase Offensive, which they executed at two sectors: in the East at the Chosin Reservoir and in the Western sector at Ch'ongch'on River.

On 13 November, Mao appointed Zhou Enlai the overall commander and coordinator of the war effort, with Peng as field commander.

On 25 November, on the Korean western front, the PVA 13th Army Group attacked and overran the ROK II Corps at the Battle of the Ch'ongch'on River, and then inflicted heavy losses on the U.S. 2nd Infantry Division on the UN forces' right flank.

Believing that they could not hold against the PVA, the Eighth Army began to retreat from North Korea crossing the 38th Parallel in mid-December.

UN morale hit rock bottom when Lieutenant General Walton Walker, commander of the U.S. Eighth Army, was killed on 23 December 1950 in an automobile accident.

In the east, on 27 November, the PVA 9th Army Group initiated the Battle of Chosin Reservoir. Here, the UN forces fared comparatively better: like the Eighth Army, the surprise attack also forced X Corps to retreat from northeast Korea, but they were, in the process, able to break out from the attempted encirclement by the PVA and execute a successful tactical withdrawal.

X Corps managed to establish a defensive perimeter at the port city of Hungnam on 11 December and were able to evacuate by 24 December to reinforce the badly depleted U.S. Eighth Army to the south.

During the evacuation, about 193 shiploads of UN forces and matériel, approximately 105,000 soldiers, 98,000 civilians, 17,500 vehicles, and 350,000 tons of supplies) were evacuated to Pusan.

The SS Meredith Victory was noted for evacuating 14,000 refugees, the largest rescue operation by a single ship, even though it was designed to hold 12 passengers. Before escaping, the UN forces razed most of Hungnam city, with particular attention to the port facilities.

The UN retreat from North Korea also saw the massive evacuation from the capital city of Pyongyang. In early December, UN forces, including the British Army's 29th Infantry Brigade, evacuated Pyongyang, along with large numbers of refugees.

Around 4.5 million North Koreans are estimated to have fled from North Korea to either the South or elsewhere abroad.

On 16 December 1950, President Truman declared a national state of emergency with Presidential Proclamation No. 2914, 3 C.F.R. 99, 1953, which remained in force until 14 September 1978.

The next day, 17 December 1950, Kim Il Sung was deprived of the right of command of KPA by China.

China justified its entry into the war as a response to what it described as "American aggression in the guise of the UN".

Chinese decision-makers feared that the American-led invasion of North Korea was part of a U.S. strategy to invade China ultimately. They were also worried about rising counterrevolutionary activity at home.

MacArthur's public statements that he wanted to extend the Korean War into China and return the Kuomintang to power reinforced this fear. Later, the Chinese claimed that U.S. bombers had violated PRC national airspace on three separate occasions and attacked Chinese targets before China intervened.

CHAPTER 20

Fighting around the 38th Parallel
January–June 1951

A ceasefire presented by the UN to the PRC shortly after the Battle of the Ch'ongch'on River on 11 December 1950, was rejected by the Chinese government, which was convinced of the PVA's invincibility after its victory in that battle and the wider Second Phase Offensive and wanted to demonstrate China's desire for a total victory through the expulsion of the UN forces from Korea.

With Lieutenant General Matthew Ridgway assuming the command of the U.S. Eighth Army on 26 December, the PVA and the KPA launched their Third Phase Offensive, also known as the "Chinese New Year's Offensive", on New Year's Eve of 1950/51.

Utilizing night attacks in which UN fighting positions were encircled and then assaulted by numerically superior troops who had the element of surprise, the attacks were accompanied by loud trumpets and gongs, which fulfilled the double purpose of facilitating tactical communication and mentally disorienting the enemy. UN forces initially had no familiarity with this tactic, and as a result, some soldiers panicked, abandoning their weapons, and retreating to the south.

The offensive overwhelmed UN forces, allowing the PVA and KPA to capture Seoul for the second time on 4 January 1951. Following this, the CPV party committee issued orders regarding tasks during rest and reorganization on 8 January 1951, outlining Chinese war goals. The orders read: "the central issue is for the whole party and army to overcome difficulties… to improve tactics and skills.

When the next campaign starts… we will annihilate all enemies and liberate all Korea." In his telegram to Peng on 14 January, Mao stressed the importance of preparing for "the last battle" in the spring to "fundamentally resolve the Korean issue".

B-26 Invaders bomb logistics depots in Wonsan, North Korea, 1951

These setbacks prompted General MacArthur to consider using nuclear weapons against the Chinese or North Korean interiors, intending radioactive fallout zones to interrupt the Chinese supply chains.

However, upon the arrival of the charismatic General Ridgway, the esprit de corps of the bloodied Eighth Army immediately began to revive.

UN forces retreated to Suwon in the west, Wonju in the center, and the territory north of Samcheok in the east, where the battlefront stabilized and held.

The PVA had outrun its logistics capability and thus were unable to press on beyond Seoul as food, ammunition, and matériel were carried nightly, on foot and bicycle, from the border at the Yalu River to the three battle lines.

In late January, upon finding that the PVA had abandoned their battle lines, General Ridgway ordered a reconnaissance-in-force, which became Operation Thunderbolt, 25 January 1951.

A full-scale advance followed, which fully exploited the UN's air superiority, concluding with the UN forces reaching the Han River and recapturing Wonju.

Following the failure of ceasefire negotiations in January, the United Nations General Assembly passed Resolution 498 on 1 February, condemning the PRC as an aggressor, and called upon its forces to withdraw from Korea.

In early February, the ROK 11th Division ran an operation to destroy guerrillas and pro-DPRK sympathizers in Southern Korea.

During the operation, the division and police conducted the Geochang massacre and San Cheong–Hamyang massacre.

In mid-February, the PVA counterattacked with the Fourth Phase Offensive and achieved initial victory at Hoengseong. However, the offensive was soon blunted by U.S. IX Corps at Chipyong-ni in the center.

The U.S. 23rd Regimental Combat Team and the French Battalion fought a short but desperate battle that broke the attack's momentum.

The battle is sometimes known as the "Gettysburg of the Korean War": 5,600 U.S., and French troops were surrounded on all sides, by 25,000 PVA. UN forces had previously retreated in the face of large PVA/KPA forces instead of getting cut surrounded.

In the last two weeks of February 1951, Operation Thunderbolt was followed by Operation Killer, carried out by the revitalized Eighth Army. It was a full-scale, battlefront-length attack staged for maximum exploitation of firepower to kill as many KPAS and PVA troops as possible.

Operation Killer concluded with U.S. I Corps re-occupying the territory south of the Han River, and IX Corps capturing Hoengseong.

On 7 March 1951, the Eighth Army attacked with Operation Ripper, expelling the PVA and the KPA from Seoul on 14 March 1951.

This was the fourth and final conquest of the city in a year's time, leaving it a ruin; the 1.5 million pre-war population was down to 200,000, and people were suffering from severe food shortages.

On 1 March 1951, Mao sent a cable to Stalin emphasizing the difficulties faced by Chinese forces and the need for air cover, especially over supply lines.

Apparently impressed by the Chinese war effort, Stalin agreed to supply two air force divisions, three anti-aircraft divisions, and six thousand trucks.

PVA troops in Korea continued to suffer severe logistical problems throughout the war. In late April, Peng Dehuai sent his deputy, Hong Xuezhi, to brief Zhou Enlai in Beijing.

What Chinese soldiers feared, Hong said, was not the enemy, but having no food, bullets, or trucks to transport them to the rear when they were wounded.

Zhou attempted to respond to the PVA's logistical concerns by increasing Chinese production and improving supply methods, but these efforts were never sufficient.

At the same time, large-scale air defense training programs were carried out, and the People's Liberation Army Air Force, PLAAF, began participating in the war from September 1951 onward.

The Fourth Phase Offensive had catastrophically failed, in contrast to the success of the Second Phase Offensive and limited gains of the Third Phase Offensive.

The UN forces, after earlier defeats and subsequent retraining, proved much harder to infiltrate by Chinese light infantry than they had been in previous months. From 31 January to 21 April, the Chinese had suffered 53,000 casualties.

On 11 April 1951, President Truman relieved General MacArthur as Supreme Commander in Korea.

There were several reasons for the dismissal. MacArthur had crossed the 38th Parallel in the mistaken belief that the Chinese would not enter the war, leading to major allied losses.

He believed that the use of nuclear weapons should be his decision, not the President's. MacArthur threatened to destroy China unless it surrendered.

While MacArthur felt total victory was the only honorable outcome, Truman was more pessimistic about his chances once involved in a larger war, feeling that a truce and orderly withdrawal from Korea could be a valid solution.

MacArthur was the subject of congressional hearings in May and June 1951, which determined that he had defied the orders of the President and thus had violated the U.S. Constitution.

A popular criticism of MacArthur was that he never spent a night in Korea and directed the war from the safety of Tokyo.

CHAPTER 21

British UN troops advance alongside a Centurion tank, March 1951

MacArthur was relieved primarily due to his determination to expand the war into China, which other officials believed would needlessly escalate a limited war and consume too many already overstretched resources.

Despite MacArthur's claims that he was restricted to fighting a limited war when China was fighting all-out, congressional testimony revealed China was using restraint as much as the U.S. was, as they were not using air power against front-line troops, communication lines, ports, naval air forces, or staging bases in Japan, which had been crucial to the survival of UN forces in Korea.

Simply fighting on the peninsula had already tied down significant portions of U.S. airpower; as Air Force chief of staff Hoyt Vandenberg said, 80–85% of the tactical capacity, one-fourth of the strategic portion, and 20% of air defense forces of the USAF were engaged in a single country.

There was also fear that crossing into China would provoke the Soviet Union into entering the war. General Omar Bradley testified that there were 35 Russian divisions totaling some 500,000 troops in the Far East, and if sent into action with the approximately 85 Russian submarines in the vicinity of Korea, they could overwhelm U.S. forces and cut supply lines, as well as potentially assist China in taking over territory in Southeast Asia.

General Ridgway was appointed Supreme Commander in Korea, and he regrouped the UN forces for successful counterattacks, while General James Van Fleet assumed command of the U.S. Eighth Army.

Further attacks slowly depleted the PVA and KPA forces; Operations Courageous 23–28 March 1951 and Tomahawk, 23 March 1951, a combat jump by the 187th Airborne Regimental Combat Team, were a joint ground and airborne infiltration meant to trap PVA forces between Kaesong and Seoul. UN forces advanced to the Kansas Line, north of the 38th Parallel.

The PVA counterattacked in April 1951, with the Fifth Phase Offensive, with three field armies, approximately 700,000 men.

The first thrust of the offensive fell upon I Corps, which fiercely resisted in the Battle of the Imjin River, 22–25 April 1951, and the Battle of Kapyong, 22–25 April 195), blunting the impetus of the offensive, which was halted at the No-name Line north of Seoul.

Casualty ratios were grievously disproportionate; Peng had expected a 1–1 or 2-1 ratio, but instead, Chinese combat casualties from 22 to 29 April totaled between 40,000 and 60,000 compared to only 4,000 for the UN —a casualty ratio between 10–1 and 15–1.

By the time Peng had called off the attack in the western sector on 29 April, the three participating armies had lost a third of their front-line combat strength within a week.

Additional casualties were incurred on 30 April. On 15 May 1951, the PVA commenced the second impulse of the Spring Offensive and attacked the ROK and U.S. X Corps in the east at the Soyang River.

Approximately 370,000 PVA and 114,000 KPA troops had been mobilized for the second step of the Fifth Phase Offensive, with the bulk attacking in the eastern sector with about a quarter attempting to pin the U.S. I Corps and IX Corps in the western sector.

After initial success, they were halted by 20 May and repulsed over the following days, with Western histories generally designating 22 May as the end of the offensive.

At month's end, the Chinese planned the third step of the Fifth Phase Offensive, withdrawal, which they estimated would take 10 to 15 days to complete for their 340,000 remaining men and set the retreat date for the night of 23 May.

They were caught off guard when the U.S. Eighth Army counterattacked and regained the Kansas Line on the morning of 12 May, 23 hours before the expected withdrawal.

The surprise attack turned the retreat into "the most severe loss since our forces had entered Korea"; from 16 May to 23 May, the PVA had suffered another 45,000 to 60,000 casualties before their remaining soldiers managed to evacuate back north.

Per official Chinese statistics, the Fifth Phase Offensive had cost the PVA 102,000 soldiers (85,000 killed/wounded, 17,000 captured), with unknown but significant losses for the KPA.

The end of the Fifth Phase Offensive preceded the start of the UN May–June 1951 counteroffensive. During the counteroffensive, the U.S.-led coalition captured land up to about 10 km (6 mi) north of the 38th Parallel, with most forces stopping at the Kansas Line and a minority going further to the Wyoming Line.

PVA and KPA forces suffered greatly during this offensive, especially in the Chuncheon sector and at Chiam-ni and Hwacheon; in the latter sector alone the PVA/KPA suffered over 73,207 casualties, including 8,749 captured, compared to 2,647 total casualties of the U.S. IX Corps which engaged them.

The UN's Kansas Line halt and subsequent offensive action stand-down began the stalemate that lasted until the armistice of 1953.

The disastrous failure of the Fifth Phase Offensive, which Peng later recalled as one of only four mistakes he made in his military career, "led Chinese leaders to change their goal from driving the UNF out of Korea to merely defending China's security and ending the war through negotiations".

CHAPTER 22

Stalemate July 1951 – July 1953

For the remainder of the war, the UN and the PVA/KPA fought but exchanged little territory, as the stalemate held.

Large-scale bombing of North Korea continued, and protracted armistice negotiations began on 10 July 1951 at Kaesong, an ancient capital of Korea located in PVA/KPA held territory.

On the Chinese side, Zhou Enlai directed peace talks, and Li Kenong and Qiao Guanghua headed the negotiation team.

Combat continued while the belligerents negotiated; the goal of the UN forces was to recapture all South Korea and to avoid losing territory.

The PVA and the KPA attempted similar operations and later effected military and psychological operations to test the UN Command's resolve to continue the war.

The two sides constantly traded artillery fire along the front, with American-led forces possessing a large firepower advantage over the Chinese-led forces.

For example, in the last three months of 1952 the UN fired 3,553,518 field gun shells and 2,569,941 mortar shells, while the Communists fired 377,782 field gun shells and 672,194 mortar shells: an overall 5.83:1 ratio in the UN's favor.

The Communist insurgency, reinvigorated by North Korean support and scattered bands of KPA stragglers, also resurged in the south.

In the autumn of 1951, Van Fleet ordered Major General Paik Sun-yup to break the back of guerrilla activity. From December 1951 to March 1952, ROK security forces claimed to have killed 11,090 partisans and sympathizers and captured 9,916 more.

CHAPTER 23

U.S. M46 Patton tanks, painted with tiger heads thought to demoralize Chinese forces

The principal battles of the stalemate include the Battle of Bloody Ridge, 18 August–15 September 1951, the Battle of the Punchbowl, 31 August-21 September 1951, the Battle of Heartbreak Ridge, 13 September–15 October 1951, the Battle of Old Baldy, 26 June–4 August 1952, the Battle of White Horse, 6–15 October 1952, the Battle of Triangle Hill, 14 October–25 November 1952, the Battle of Hill Eerie, 21 March–21 June 1952, the sieges of Outpost Harry, 10–18 June 1953, the Battle of the Hook, 28–29 May 1953, the Battle of Pork Chop Hill, 23 March–16 July 1953, and the Battle of Kumsong, 13–27 July 1953.

PVA troops suffered from deficient military equipment, serious logistical problems, overextended communication and supply lines, and the constant threat of UN bombers.

All these factors generally led to a rate of Chinese casualties that was far greater than the casualties suffered by UN troops. The situation became so serious that, in November 1951, Zhou Enlai called a conference in Shenyang to discuss the PVA's logistical problems.

At the meeting, it was decided to accelerate the construction of railways and airfields in the area to increase the number of trucks available to the army, and to improve air defense by any means possible.

These commitments did little to address the problems directly that confronted PVA troops.

CHAPTER 24

New Zealand artillery crew in action, 1952

In the months after the Shenyang conference, Peng Dehuai went to Beijing several times to brief Mao and Zhou about the heavy casualties suffered by Chinese troops and the increasing difficulty of keeping the front lines supplied with necessities. Peng was convinced that the war would be protracted and that neither side would be able to achieve victory soon.

On 24 February 1952, the Military Commission, presided over by Zhou, discussed the PVA's logistical problems with members of various government agencies involved in the war effort.

After the government representatives emphasized their inability to meet the demands of the war, Peng, in an angry outburst, shouted: "You have this and that problem.

You should go to the front and see with your own eyes what food and clothing the soldiers have! Not to speak of the casualties! For what are they giving their lives? We have no aircraft. We have only a few guns.

Transport is not protected. More and more soldiers are dying of starvation. Can't you overcome some of your difficulties?" The atmosphere became so tense that Zhou was forced to adjourn the conference.

Zhou subsequently called a series of meetings, where it was agreed that the PVA would be divided into three groups, to be dispatched to Korea in shifts; to accelerate the training of Chinese pilots; to provide more anti-aircraft guns to the front lines; to purchase more military equipment and ammunition from the Soviet Union; to provide the army with more food and clothing; and to transfer the responsibility of logistics to the central government.

With peace negotiations ongoing, the Chinese attempted one final offensive in the final weeks of the war to capture territory: on 10 June, 30,000 Chinese troops struck two South Korean and one U.S. divisions on a 13 km (8 mi) front, and on 13 July, 80,000 Chinese soldiers struck the east central Kumsong sector, with the brunt of their attack falling on four South Korean divisions.

In both cases, the Chinese had some success in penetrating South Korean lines, but failed to capitalize, particularly when the U.S. forces present responded with overwhelming firepower.

Chinese casualties in their final major offensive of the war (above normal wastage for the front) were about 72,000, including 25,000 killed in action compared to 14,000 for the UN, most of these deaths were South Koreans, though 1,611 were Americans. The Communists fired 704,695 field gun shells in June–July compared to 4,711,230 fired by the UN, a ratio of 1:6.69.

June 1953 saw the highest monthly artillery expenditure of the war by both sides.

CHAPTER 25

Armistice July 1953 – November 1954

Korean Armistice Agreement
Men from the Royal Australian Regiment, June 1953

The on-again, off-again armistice negotiations continued for two years, first at Kaesong, on the border between North and South Korea, and then at the neighboring village of Panmunjom.

A major, problematic negotiation point was prisoner of war (POW) repatriation. The PVA, KPA and UN Command could not agree on a system of repatriation because many PVA and KPA soldiers refused to be repatriated back to the north, which was unacceptable to the Chinese and North Koreans.[

A Neutral Nations Repatriation Commission, under the chairman Indian General K. S. Thimayya, was subsequently set up to handle the matter.

In 1952, the U.S. elected a new president, and on 29 November 1952, the president-elect, Dwight D. Eisenhower, went to Korea to learn what might end the Korean War.

Eisenhower took office on 20 January 1953. Joseph Stalin died a few weeks later 5 March. The new Soviet leaders, engaged in their internal power struggle, had no desire to continue supporting China's efforts in Korea, and issued a statement calling for an end to the hostilities.

China could not continue the war without Soviet aid and North Korea was no longer a major player. Armistice talks entered a new phase. With the United Nations' acceptance of India's proposed Korean War armistice, the KPA, the PVA and the UN Command signed the Korean Armistice Agreement on 27 July 1953.

South Korean president Syngman Rhee refused to sign the agreement. The war is considered to have ended at this point, even though there was no peace treaty. North Korea nevertheless claims that it won the Korean War.

Under the Armistice Agreement, the belligerents established the Korean Demilitarized Zone (DMZ), along the front line, which vaguely follows the 38th Parallel. In the eastern part, the DMZ runs north of the 38th Parallel; to the west, it travels south of it.

Kaesong, site of the initial armistice negotiations, was originally in pre-war South Korea but now is part of North Korea.

The DMZ has since been patrolled by the KPA and the ROK and the U.S. still operating as the UN Command.

The Armistice also called upon the governments of South Korea, North Korea, China, and the United States to participate in continued peace talks.

After the war, Operation Glory was conducted from July to November 1954, to allow combatant countries to exchange their dead. The remains of 4,167 U.S. Army and U.S. Marine Corps dead were exchanged for 13,528 KPA and PVA dead, and 546 civilians dead in UN prisoner-of-war camps were delivered to the South Korean government.

After Operation Glory, 416 Korean War unknown soldiers were buried in the National Memorial Cemetery of the Pacific, The Punchbowl, on the island of Oahu, Hawaii. Defense Prisoner of War/Missing Personnel Office (DPMO) records indicate that the PRC and North Korea transmitted 1,394 names, of which 858 were correct. From 4,167 containers of returned remains, forensic examination identified 4,219 individuals.

Of these, 2,944 were identified as from the U.S., and all but 416 were identified by name.

From 1996 to 2006, North Korea recovered 220 remains near the Sino-Korean border.

CHAPTER 26

Division of Korea 1954–present

Delegates sign the Korean Armistice Agreement in P'anmunjŏm

The Korean Armistice Agreement provided for monitoring by an international commission. Since 1953, the Neutral Nations Supervisory Commission (NNSC), composed of members from the Swiss and Swedish Armed Forces, has been stationed near the DMZ.

In April 1975, South Vietnam's capital was captured by the People's Army of Vietnam. Encouraged by the success of the Communist revolution in Indochina, Kim Il Sung saw it as an opportunity to invade the South. Kim visited China in April of that year and met with Mao Zedong and Zhou Enlai to ask for military aid.

Despite Pyongyang's expectations, however, Beijing refused to help North Korea for another war in Korea.

A U.S. Army officer confers with South Korean soldiers at Observation Post (OP) Ouellette, viewing northward, in April 2008

The DMZ as seen from the north, 2005

Since the armistice, there have been numerous incursions and acts of aggression by North Korea. From 1966 to 1969, many cross-border incursions took place in what has been referred to as the Korean DMZ Conflict or the Second Korean War.

In 1968, a North Korean commando team unsuccessfully attempted to assassinate South Korean president Park Chung Hee in the Blue House Raid. In 1976, the axe murder incident was widely publicized.

Since 1974, four incursion tunnels leading to Seoul have been uncovered. In 2010, a North Korean submarine torpedoed and sank the South Korean corvette ROKS Cheonan, resulting in the deaths of 46 sailors.

Again in 2010, North Korea fired artillery shells on Yeonpyeong Island, killing two military personnel and two civilians.

After a new wave of UN sanctions, on 11 March 2013, North Korea claimed that the armistice had become invalid.

On 13 March 2013, North Korea confirmed it ended the 1953 Armistice and declared North Korea "is not restrained by the North-South declaration on non-aggression".

On 30 March 2013, North Korea stated that it entered a "state of war" with South Korea and declared that "The long-standing situation of the Korean peninsula being neither at peace nor at war is finally over".

Speaking on 4 April 2013, the U.S. Secretary of Defense, Chuck Hagel, informed the press that Pyongyang "formally informed" the Pentagon that it "ratified" the potential use of a nuclear weapon against South Korea, Japan, and the United States of America, including Guam and Hawaii.

Hagel also stated the U.S. would deploy the Terminal High Altitude Area Defense anti-ballistic missile system to Guam, because of a credible and realistic nuclear threat from North Korea.

In 2016, it was revealed that North Korea approached the United States about conducting formal peace talks to end the war officially. While the White House agreed to secret peace talks, the plan was rejected due to North Korea's refusal to discuss nuclear disarmament as part of the terms of the treaty.

On 27 April 2018, it was announced that North Korea and South Korea agreed to talks to end the ongoing 65-year conflict. They committed themselves to the complete denuclearization of the Korean Peninsula.

North Korean leader Kim Jong Un and South Korean President Moon Jae-In signed the Panmunjom Declaration for Peace, Prosperity, and Reunification of the Korean Peninsula.

On 22 September 2021, South Korean President Moon Jae-In reiterated his call to end the Korean War formally, in his speech at the United Nations General Assembly.

Casualties

Approximately 3 million people died in the Korean War, the majority of whom were civilians, making it perhaps the deadliest conflict of the Cold War era.

Samuel S. Kim lists the Korean War as the deadliest conflict in East Asia, itself the region most affected by armed conflict related to the Cold War, from 1945 to 1994, with 3 million dead, more than the Vietnam War and Chinese Civil War during the same period.

Although only rough estimates of civilian fatalities are available, scholars from Guenter Lewy to Bruce Cummings have noted that the percentage of civilian casualties in Korea was higher than in World War II or the Vietnam War, with Cummings putting civilian casualties at 2 million and Lewy estimating civilian deaths in the range of 2 million to 3 million.

Cummings states that civilians represent "at least" half of the war's casualties, while Lewy suggests that the civilian portion of the death toll "may have gone as high as 70 percent", compared to Lewy's estimates of 42% in World War II and 30%–46% in the Vietnam War.

Data compiled by the Peace Research Institute Oslo, PRIO, lists just under 1 million "battle deaths" over the course of the Korean War, with a range of 644,696 to 1.5 million, and a mid-value estimate of 3 million total death, with a range of 1.5 million to 4.5 million, attributing the difference to excess mortality among civilians from one-sided massacres, starvation, and disease.

Compounding this devastation for Korean civilians, virtually all the major cities on the entire Korean Peninsula were destroyed because of the war.

In both per capita and absolute terms, North Korea was the country most devastated by the war. According to Charles K. Armstrong, the war resulted in the death of an estimated 12%–15% of the North Korean population (c. 10 million), "a figure close to or surpassing the proportion of Soviet citizens killed in World War II".

CHAPTER 27

Military

Korean War memorials are found in every UN Command Korean War participant country; this one is in Pretoria, South Africa.

See also: Australia, Belgium and Luxembourg, Canada, Colombia, Ethiopia, France, Greece, Netherlands, New Zealand, Philippines, Thailand, Turkey, South Africa, United Kingdom, and United States.

According to the data from the U.S. Department of Defense, the U.S. suffered 33,686 battle deaths, along with 2,830 non-battle deaths during the Korean War. There were 17,730 other non-battle U.S. military deaths that occurred outside Korea during the same period that were erroneously included as Korean War deaths until 2000.

In addition, the U.S. suffered 103,284 wounded in action.

The United Nations losses, excluding those of the United States or South Korea, amounted to 4,141 dead and 12,044 wounded in action.

American combat casualties were over 90 percent of non-Korean UN losses. U.S. battle deaths were 8,516 up to their first engagement with the Chinese on 1 November 1950.

The first four months of the Korean War, that is, the war prior to the Chinese intervention, which started near the end of October, were by far the bloodiest per day for the U.S. forces as they engaged and destroyed the comparatively well-equipped KPA in intense fighting.

American medical records show that from July to October 1950, the U.S. Army sustained 31 percent of the combat deaths it ultimately incurred in the entire 37-month war.

The U.S. spent U.S.$30 billion in total on the war.[338] Some 1,789,000 American soldiers served in the Korean War, accounting for 31 percent of the 5,720,000 Americans who served on active duty worldwide from June 1950 to July 1953.

South Korea reported some 137,899 military deaths and 24,495 missing. Deaths from the other non-American UN militaries totaled 3,730, with another 379 missing.

Data from official Chinese sources reported that the PVA had suffered 114,000 battle deaths, 21,000 deaths from wounds, 13,000 deaths from illness, 340,000 wounded, and 7,600 missing during the war. 7,110 Chinese POWs were repatriated to China.

In 2010, the Chinese government revised their official tally of war losses to 183,108 dead, 114,084 in combat, 70,000 deaths from wounds, illness, and other causes, and 25,621 missing.

Overall, 73 percent of Chinese infantry troops served in Korea, 25 of 34 armies, or 79 of 109 infantry divisions, were rotated in.

More than 52 percent of the Chinese air force, 55 percent of the tank units, 67 percent of the artillery divisions, and 100 percent of the railroad engineering divisions were sent to Korea as well.

Chinese soldiers who served in Korea faced a greater chance of being killed than those who served in World War II or the Chinese Civil War.

In terms of financial cost, China spent over 10 billion yuan on the war, roughly U.S.$3.3 billion, not counting USSR aid that had been donated or forgiven. This included $1.3 billion in money owed to the Soviet Union by the end of it.

This was a relatively large cost, as China had only 1/25 the national income of the United States. Spending on the Korean War constituted 34–43 percent of China's annual government budget from 1950 to 1953, depending on the year.

Despite its underdeveloped economy, Chinese military spending was the world's fourth largest globally for most of the war after that of the United States, the Soviet Union, and the United Kingdom; however, by 1953, with the winding down of the Korean War, which ended halfway through the year, and the escalation of the FirstIndochina War, which reached its peak in 1953–1954, French spending also surpassed Chinese spending by about a third.

According to the South Korean Ministry of National Defense, North Korean military losses totaled 294,151 dead, 91,206 missing, and 229,849 wounded, giving North Korea the highest military deaths of any belligerent in both absolute and relative terms.

The PRIO Battle Deaths Dataset gave a similar figure for North Korean military deaths of 316,579. Chinese sources reported similar figures for the North Korean military of 290,000 "casualties" and 90,000 captured.

The exact financial cost of the war for North Korea is unknown but was known to be massive in terms of both direct losses and lost economic activity; the country was devastated both by the cost of the war itself and the American strategic bombing campaign, which, among other things, destroyed 85 percent of North Korea's buildings and 95 percent of its power generation capacity.

The Chinese and North Koreans estimated that about 390,000 soldiers from the United States, 660,000 soldiers from South Korea and 29,000 other UN soldiers were "eliminated" from the battlefield.

Western sources estimate the PVA suffered about 400,000 killed and 486,000 wounded, while the KPA suffered 215,000 killed, 303,000 wounded, and over 101,000 captured or missing. Cummings cites a much higher figure of 900,000 fatalities among Chinese soldiers.

Civilian

According to the South Korean Ministry of National Defense, there were over three-quarters of a million confirmed violent civilians deaths during the war, another million civilians were pronounced missing, and millions more ended up as refugees.

In South Korea, some 373,500 civilians were killed, more than 225,600 wounded, and over 387,740 were listed as missing. During the first communist occupation of Seoul alone, the KPA massacred 128,936 civilians and deported another 84,523 to North Korea.

On the other side of the border, some 1,594,000 North Koreans were reported as casualties including 406,000 civilians reported as killed, and 680,000 missing. Over 1.5 million North Koreans fled to the South during the war.

U.S. unpreparedness

In a postwar analysis of the unpreparedness of U.S. Army forces deployed to Korea during the summer and fall of 1950, Army Major General Floyd L. Parks stated that "Many who never lived to tell the tale had to fight the full range of ground warfare from offensive to delaying action, unit by unit, man by man.

That we were able to snatch victory from the jaws of defeat does not relieve us from the blame of having placed our own flesh and blood in such a predicament."

CHAPTER 28

A soldier of the Dutch Detachment of the UN forces in North Korea prepares to return sniper fire, 1952

By 1950, U.S. Secretary of Defense Louis A. Johnson had established a policy of faithfully following President Truman's defense economization plans and had aggressively attempted to implement it even in the face of steadily increasing external threats.

He consequently received much of the blame for the initial setbacks in Korea and the widespread reports of ill-equipped and inadequately trained U.S. military forces in the war's early stages.

As an initial response to the invasion, Truman called for a naval blockade of North Korea and was shocked to learn that such a blockade could be imposed only "on paper" since the U.S. Navy no longer had the warships with which to carry out his request.

Army officials, desperate for weaponry, recovered Sherman tanks and other equipment from World War II Pacific battlefields and reconditioned them for shipment to Korea.

Army Ordnance officials at Fort Knox pulled down M26 Pershing tanks from display pedestals around Fort Knox to equip the third company of the Army's hastily formed 70th Tank Battalion.

Without adequate numbers of tactical fighter-bomber aircraft, the Air Force took F-51, P-51, propeller-driven aircraft out of storage or from existing Air National Guard squadrons and rushed them into front-line service.

A shortage of spare parts and qualified maintenance personnel resulted in improvised repairs and overhauls.

A Navy helicopter pilot aboard an active-duty warship recalled fixing damaged rotor blades with masking tape in the absence of spares.

U.S. Army Reserve and Army National Guard infantry soldiers and new inductees, called to duty to fill out understrength infantry divisions, found themselves short of nearly everything needed to repel the North Korean forces: artillery, ammunition, heavy tanks, ground-support aircraft, even effective anti-tank weapons such as the M20 3.5-inch (89 mm) "Super Bazooka".

Some Army combat units sent to Korea were supplied with worn-out, "red-lined" M1 rifles or carbines in immediate need of ordnance depot overhaul or repair.

Only the Marine Corps, whose commanders had stored and maintained their World War II surplus inventories of equipment and weapons, proved ready for deployment, though they still were woefully understrength, as well as in need of suitable landing craft to practice amphibious operations, Secretary of Defense Louis Johnson had transferred most of the remaining craft to the Navy and reserved them for use in training Army units.

Due to public criticism of his handling of the Korean War, Truman decided to ask for Johnson's resignation. On 19 September 1950, Johnson resigned as Secretary of Defense, and the president quickly replaced him with General George C. Marshall.

Armored warfare

The initial assault by KPA forces was aided using Soviet T-34-85 tanks. A KPA tank corps equipped with about 120 T-34s spearheaded the invasion. These faced an ROK that had few anti-tank weapons adequate to deal with the T-34s.

Additional Soviet armor was added as the offensive progressed. The KPA tanks had a good deal of early successes against ROK infantry, Task Force Smith, and the U.S. M24 Chaffee light tanks that they encountered.

Interdiction by ground attack aircraft was the only means of slowing the advancing KPA armor.

The tide turned in favor of the UN forces in August 1950 when the KPA suffered major tank losses during a series of battles in which the UN forces brought heavier equipment to bear, including M4A3 Sherman and M26 medium tanks, as well as the British Centurion, Churchill, and Cromwell tanks.

The Incheon landings on 15 September cut off the KPA supply lines, causing their armored forces and infantry to run out of fuel, ammunition, and other supplies.

As a result of this and the Pusan perimeter breakout, the KPA had to retreat, and many of the T-34s and heavy weapons had to be abandoned. By the time the KPA withdrew from the South, a total of 239 T-34s and 74 SU-76 self-propelled guns were lost. After November 1950, KPA armor was rarely encountered.

Following the initial assault by the North, the Korean War saw limited use of tanks and featured no large-scale tank battles. The mountainous, forested terrain, especially in the eastern central zone, was a poor tank country, limiting their mobility. Through the last two years of the war in Korea, UN tanks served largely as infantry support and mobile artillery pieces.

CHAPTER 29

Naval warfare

Naval engagements of the Korean War (1950–1953) and post-armistice incidents

To disrupt North Korean communications, USS Missouri fires a salvo from its 16-inch guns at shore targets near Chongjin, North Korea, 21 October 1950.

Because neither of Korea had a significant navy, the war featured few naval battles. A skirmish between North Korea and the UN Command occurred on 2 July 1950; the U.S. Navy cruiser USS Juneau, the Royal Navy cruiser HMS Jamaica and the Royal Navy frigate HMS Black Swan fought four North Korean torpedo boats and two mortar gunboats and sank them.

USS Juneau later sank several ammunition ships that had been present. The last sea battle of the Korean War occurred days before the Battle of Incheon; the ROK ship PC-703 sank a North Korean minelayer in the Battle of Haeju Island, near Incheon.

Three other supply ships were sunk by PC-703 two days later in the Yellow Sea.

Thereafter, vessels from the UN nations held undisputed control of the sea about Korea. The gunships were used in shore bombardment, while the aircraft carriers provided air support to the ground forces.

During most of the war, the UN navies patrolled the west and east coasts of North Korea, sinking supply and ammunition ships and denying the North Koreans the ability to resupply from the sea. Aside from very occasional gunfire from North Korean shore batteries, the main threat to UN navy ships was from magnetic mines.

During the war, five U.S. Navy ships were lost to mines: two minesweepers, two minesweeper escorts, and one ocean tug. Mines and gunfire from North Korean coastal artillery damaged another 87 U.S. warships, resulting in slight to moderate damage.

Aerial warfare

MiG Alley, USAF Units and Aircraft of the Korean War, and Korean People's Air Force

The war was the first in which jet aircraft played the central role in air combat. Once-formidable fighters such as the P-51 Mustang, F4U Corsair, and Hawker Sea Fury all piston-engine, propeller-driven, and designed during World War II, relinquished their air-superiority roles to a new generation of faster, jet-powered fighters arriving in the theater.

For the initial months of the war, the P-80 Shooting Star, F9F Panther, Gloster Meteor, and other jets under the UN flag dominated the Korean People's Air Force (KPAF) propeller-driven Soviet Yakovlev Yak-9 and Lavochkin La-9 By early August 1950, the KPAF was reduced to only about 20 planes.

The Chinese intervention in late October 1950 bolstered the KPAF with the MiG-15, one of the world's most advanced jet fighters.

The heavily armed MiGs were faster than first-generation UN jets and therefore could reach and destroy U.S. B-29 Superfortress bomber flights despite their fighter escorts. With increasing B-29 losses, the USAF was forced to switch from daylight bombing to safer but less accurate nighttime bombing.

The USAF countered the MiG-15 by sending over three squadrons of its most capable fighter, the F-86 Sabre. These arrived in December 1950.

The Soviet Union denied the involvement of their personnel in anything other than an advisory role, but air combat quickly resulted in Soviet pilots dropping their code signals and speaking over the radio in Russian.

This known direct Soviet participation was a casus bello that the UN Command deliberately overlooked, lest the war expand to include the Soviet Union, and potentially escalate into atomic warfare.

After the war, and to the present day, the USAF reported an inflated F-86 Sabre kill ratio more than 10:1, with 792 MiG-15s and 108 other aircraft shot down by Sabres, and 78 Sabres lost to enemy fire.

The Soviet Air Force reported some 1,100 air-to-air victories and 335 MiG combat losses, while China's PLAAF reported 231 combat losses, mostly MiG-15s, and 168 other aircraft lost.

The KPAF reported no data, but the UN Command estimates some 200 KPAF aircraft lost in the war's first stage, and 70 additional aircraft after the Chinese intervention. The USAF disputes Soviet and Chinese claims of 650 and 211 downed F-86s, respectively.

More modern estimates place the overall USAF kill ratio at around 1.8:1 with the ratio dropping to 1.3:1 against MiG-15s with Soviet pilots but increasing to a dominant 12:1 against Chinese and North Korean adversaries.

Reports by Lt. Gen. Sidor Slyusarev, commander of Soviet air forces in Korea are more favorable to the Communist side.

The 64th Corps claimed a total of 1,097 enemy aircraft of all types during operations, for the loss of 335 aircraft, including lost to enemy ground fire, accidents, etc. and 110 pilots. Soviet reports put the overall kill ratio at 3.4:1 in favor of Soviet pilots.

As reported, the effectiveness of the Soviet fighters declined as the war progressed. from an overall kill ratio of 7.9:1 from November 1950 through January 1952, declining to 2.2:1 in later 1952 and 1.9:1 in 1953.

This was due in part to more advanced jet fighters appearing on the UN side and improving U.S. tactics.

Regardless of the actual ratio, American Sabres were very effective at controlling the skies over Korea. Since no other UN fighter could contend with the MiG-15, F-86s largely took over air combat once they arrived, relegating other aircraft to air-to-ground operations.

Despite much greater numbers. The number of Sabres in theater never exceeded 150 while MiG-15s reached 900 at their peak, Communist aircraft were seldom encountered south of Pyongyang.

UN ground forces, supply lines, and infrastructure were not attacked from the air. Although North Korea had 75 airfields capable of supporting MiGs, after 1951, any serious effort to operate from them was abandoned.

The MiGs were instead based across the Yalu River in the safety of China. This confined most air-to-air engagements to MiG Alley. UN aircraft had free rein to conduct strike missions over enemy territory with little fear of interception.

Although jet dogfights are remembered as a prominent part of the Korean War, counter-air missions comprised just 12% of Far East Air Forces sorties, and four times as many sorties were performed for close air support and interdiction.

The war marked a major milestone not only for fixed-wing aircraft, but also for rotorcraft, featuring the first large-scale deployment of helicopters for medical evacuation, medevac.

In 1944–1945, during World War II, the YR-4 helicopter had seen limited ambulance duty. In Korea, where rough terrain prevented use of the jeep as a speedy medevac vehicle, helicopters like the Sikorsky H-19 were heavily used.

This helped reduce fatal casualties to a dramatic degree when combined with complementary medical innovations such as Mobile Army Surgical Hospitals.

As such, the medical evacuation and care system for the wounded was so effective for the UN forces that a wounded soldier who arrived at a MASH unit alive typically had a 97% chance of survival.

The limitations of jet aircraft for close air support highlighted the helicopter's potential in the role, leading to the development of the helicopter gunships used in the Vietnam War 1965–1975.

CHAPTER 30

Bombing of North Korea

Pyongyang in May 1951

The initial bombing attack on North Korea was approved on the fourth day of the war, 29 June 1950, by General Douglas MacArthur immediately upon request by the commanding general of the Far East Air Forces (FEAF), George E. Stratemeyer.

Major bombing began in late July. U.S. airpower conducted 7,000 close support and interdiction airstrikes that month, which helped slow the North Korean rate of advance to 3 km (2 mi) a day.

On 12 August 1950, the USAF dropped 625 tons of bombs on North Korea, two weeks later, the daily tonnage increased to some 800 tons.

From June through October, official U.S. policy was to pursue precision bombing aimed at communication centers, railroad stations, marshaling yards, main yards, and railways and industrial facilities deemed vital to war-making capacity.

The policy was the result of debates after World War II, in which U.S. policy rejected the mass civilian bombings that had been conducted in the later stages of World War II as unproductive and immoral.

In early July, General Emmett O'Donnell Jr. requested permission to firebomb five North Korean cities. He proposed that MacArthur announce that the UN would employ the firebombing methods that "brought Japan to its knees".

The announcement would warn the leaders of North Korea "to get women and children and other noncombatants the hell out".

According to O'Donnell, MacArthur responded, "No, Rosie, I'm not prepared to go that far yet. My instructions are very explicit; however, I want you to know that I have no compunction whatever to your bombing bona fide military objectives, with high explosives, in those five industrial centers.

If you miss your target and kill people or destroy other parts of the city, I accept that as a part of war."

In September 1950, MacArthur said in his public report to the UN, "The problem of avoiding the killing of innocent civilians and damages to the civilian economy is continually present and given my personal attention."

In October 1950, FEAF commander General Stratemeyer requested permission to attack the city of Sinuiju, a provincial capital with an estimated population of 60,000, "over the widest area of the city, without warning, by burning and high explosives".

MacArthur's headquarters responded the following day: "The general policy enunciated from Washington negates such an attack unless the military situation clearly requires it. Under present circumstances this is not the case."

Following the intervention of the Chinese in November, General MacArthur ordered increased bombing on North Korea, which included firebombing against the country's arsenals and communications centers and especially against the "Korean end" of all the bridges across the Yalu River.

As with the aerial bombing campaigns over Germany and Japan in World War II, the nominal objective of the USAF was to destroy North Korea's war infrastructure and shatter the country's morale.

On 3 November 1950, General Stratemeyer forwarded to MacArthur the request of Fifth Air Force Commander General Earle E. Partridge for clearance to "burn Sinuiju".

As he had done previously in July and October, MacArthur denied the request, explaining that he planned to use the town's facilities after seizing it.

However, at the same meeting, MacArthur agreed for the first time to a firebombing campaign, agreeing to Stratemeyer request to burn the city of Kanggye and several other towns: "Burn it if you so desire.

Not only that, Strat, but burn and destroy as a lesson to any other of those towns that you consider of military value to the enemy."

The same evening, MacArthur's chief of staff told Stratemeyer that the firebombing of Sinuiju had also been approved. In his diary, Stratemeyer summarized the instructions as follows: "Every installation, facility, and village in North Korea now becomes a military and tactical target." Stratemeyer sent orders to the Fifth Air Force and Bomber Command to "destroy every means of communications and every installation, factory, city, and village".

On 5 November 1950, General Stratemeyer gave the following order to the commanding general of the Fifth Air Force: "Aircraft under Fifth Air Force control will destroy all other targets including all buildings capable of affording shelter."

The same day, twenty-two B-29s attacked Kanggye, destroying 75% of the city.

After MacArthur was removed as UN Supreme Commander in Korea in April 1951, his successors continued this policy and ultimately extended it to all North Korea.

The U.S. dropped a total of 635,000 tons of bombs, including 32,557 tons of napalm, on Korea, more than during the whole Pacific campaign of World War II.

North Korea ranks alongside Cambodia, 500,000 tons, Laos, 2 million tons and South Vietnam, 4 million tons, as among the most heavily bombed countries in history, with Laos suffering the most extensive bombardment relative to its size and population.

CHAPTER 31

A USAF Douglas B-26B Invader of the 452nd Bombardment Wing bombing a target in North Korea, 29 May 1951

Almost every substantial building in North Korea was destroyed as a result. The war's highest-Xranking U.S. POW, Major General William F. Dean, reported that most North Korean cities and villages he saw were either rubble or snow-covered wasteland.

North Korean factories, schools, hospitals, and government offices were forced to move underground, and air defenses were "non-existent".

In November 1950, the North Korean leadership instructed their population to build dugouts and mud huts and to dig tunnels to solve the acute housing problem.

U.S. Air Force General Curtis LeMay commented: "We went over there and fought the war and eventually burned down every town in North Korea anyway, some way or another, and some in South Korea, too. U.S. Colonel Dean Rusk, later secretary of state, stated the U.S. bombed "everything that moved in North Korea, every brick standing on top of another."

Pyongyang, which saw 75 percent of its area destroyed, was so devastated that bombing was halted as there were no longer any worthy targets left.

On 28 November, Bomber Command reported on the campaign's progress: 95 percent of Manpojin was destroyed, along with 90 percent of Hoeryong, Namsi and Koindong, 85 percent of Chosan, 75 percent of both Sakchu and Huichon and 20 percent of Uiju.

According to USAF damage assessments, "Eighteen of twenty-two major cities in North Korea had been at least half obliterated."

By the end of the campaign, U.S. bombers had difficulty in finding targets and were reduced to bombing footbridges or jettisoning their bombs into the sea.

In May 1953, five major North Korean dams were bombed. According to Charles K. Armstrong, the bombing of these dams and ensuing floods threatened several million North Koreans with starvation, although large-scale famine was averted with emergency aid provided by North Korea's allies.

General Matthew Ridgway said that except for air power, "the war would have been over in 60 days with all Korea in Communist hands". UN air forces flew 1,040,708 combat and combat support sorties during the war.

FEAF flew the majority at 710,886 (69.3% of sorties), with the U.S. Navy performing 16.1%, the U.S. Marine Corps 10.3%, and 4.3% by other allied air forces.

As well as conventional bombing, the Communist side claimed that the U.S. used biological weapons. These claims have been disputed; Conrad Crane asserts that while the U.S. worked towards developing chemical and biological weapons, the U.S. military "possessed neither the ability, nor the will", to use them in combat.

CHAPTER 32

U.S. threat of Atomic Warfare

Mark 4 bomb, seen on display, transferred to the 9th Bombardment Wing, Heavy On 5 November 1950, the U.S. Joint Chiefs of Staff issued orders for the retaliatory atomic bombing of Manchurian PRC military bases if either of their armies crossed into Korea or if PRC or KPA bombers attacked Korea from there.

President Truman ordered the transfer of nine Mark 4 nuclear bombs "to the Air Force's Ninth Bomb Group, the designated carrier of the weapons and signed an order to use them against Chinese and Korean targets", which he never transmitted.

Many U.S. officials viewed the deployment of nuclear-capable, but not nuclear-armed, B-29 bombers to Britain as helping to resolve the Berlin Blockade of 1948–1949. Truman and Eisenhower both had military experience and viewed nuclear weapons as potentially usable components of their military. During Truman's first meeting to discuss the war on 25 June 1950, he ordered plans be prepared for attacking Soviet forces if they entered the war.

By July, Truman approved another B-29 deployment to Britain, this time with bombs, but without their cores, to remind the Soviets of U.S. offensive ability. Deployment of a similar fleet to Guam was leaked to The New York Times.

As UN forces retreated to Pusan, and the CIA reported that mainland China was building up forces for a possible invasion of Taiwan, the Pentagon believed that Congress and the public would demand the use of nuclear weapons if the situation in Korea required them.

As PVA forces pushed back the UN forces from the Yalu River, Truman stated during a 30 November 1950 press conference that using nuclear weapons was "always [under] active consideration", with control under the local military commander.

The Indian ambassador, K. Madhava Panikkar, reports "that Truman announced he was thinking of using the atom bomb in Korea.

But the Chinese seemed unmoved by this threat... The PRC's propaganda against the U.S. was stepped up.

The 'Aid Korea to resist America' campaign was made the slogan for increased production, greater national integration, and more rigid control over anti-national activities.

One could not help feeling that Truman's threat came in useful to the leaders of the Revolution, to enable them to keep up the tempo of their activities."

After his statement caused concern in Europe, Truman met on 4 December 1950 with UK prime minister and Commonwealth spokesman Clement Attlee, French Premier René Pleven, and French Foreign Minister Robert Schuman to discuss their worries about atomic warfare and its likely continental expansion.

The U.S.' forgoing atomic warfare was not because of "a disinclination by the Soviet Union and People's Republic of China to escalate, the Korean War", but because UN allies, notably the UK, the Commonwealth, and France, were concerned about a geopolitical imbalance rendering NATO defenseless while the U.S. fought China, who then might persuade the Soviet Union to conquer Western Europe.

The Joint Chiefs of Staff advised Truman to tell Attlee that the U.S. would use nuclear weapons only if necessary to protect an evacuation of UN troops, or to prevent a "major military disaster".

On 6 December 1950, after the Chinese intervention repelled the UN armies from northern North Korea, General J. Lawton Collins, Army Chief of Staff, General MacArthur, Admiral C. Turner Joy, General George E. Stratemeyer and staff officers Major General Doyle Hickey, Major General Charles A. Willoughby and Major General Edwin K. Wright met in Tokyo to plan strategy countering the Chinese intervention; they considered three potential atomic warfare scenarios encompassing the next weeks and months of warfare.

In the first scenario: If the PVA continued attacking in full and the UN Command was forbidden to blockade and bomb China, and without Taiwanese reinforcements, and without an increase in U.S. forces until April 1951, four National Guard divisions were due to arrive, then atomic bombs might be used in North Korea.

In the second scenario: If the PVA continued full attacks and the UN Command blockaded China and had effective aerial reconnaissance and bombing of the Chinese interior, and the Taiwanese soldiers were maximally exploited, and tactical atomic bombing was to hand, then the UN forces could hold positions deep in North Korea.

In the third scenario: if China agreed not to cross the 38th Parallel border, General MacArthur recommended UN acceptance of an armistice disallowing PVA and KPA troops south of the parallel and requiring PVA and KPA guerrillas to withdraw northwards.

The U.S. Eighth Army would remain to protect the Seoul–Incheon area, while X Corps would retreat to Pusan. A UN commission should supervise the implementation of the armistice.

Both the Pentagon and the State Department were cautious about using nuclear weapons because of the risk of general war with China and the diplomatic ramifications.

Truman and his senior advisors agreed, and never seriously considered using them in early December 1950 despite the poor military situation in Korea.

In 1951, the U.S. escalated closest to atomic warfare in Korea. Because China deployed new armies to the Sino-Korean frontier, ground crews at the Kadena Air Base, Okinawa, assembled atomic bombs for Korean warfare, "lacking only the essential pit nuclear cores".

In October 1951, the United States effected Operation Hudson Harbor to establish a nuclear weapons capability. USAF B-29 bombers practiced individual bombing runs from Okinawa to North Korea, using dummy nuclear or conventional bombs, coordinated from Yokota Air Base in east-central Japan.

Hudson Harbor tested "actual functioning of all activities which would be involved in an atomic strike, including weapons assembly and testing, leading, and ground control of bomb aiming".

The bombing run data indicated that atomic bombs would be tactically ineffective against massed infantry, because the "timely identification of large masses of enemy troops was extremely rare".

General Matthew Ridgway was authorized to use nuclear weapons if a major air attack originated from outside Korea. An envoy was sent to Hong Kong to deliver a warning to China.

The message likely caused Chinese leaders to be more cautious about potential U.S. use of nuclear weapons, but whether they learned about the B-29 deployment is unclear, and the failure of the two major Chinese offensives that month likely was what caused them to shift to a defensive strategy in Korea. The B-29s returned to the United States in June.

Despite the greater destructive power that atomic weapons would bring to the war, their effects on determining the war's outcome would have likely been minimal.

Tactically, given the dispersed nature of PVA/KPA forces, the relatively primitive infrastructure for staging and logistics centers, and the small number of bombs available, most would have been conserved for use against the Soviets, atomic attacks would have limited effects against the ability of China to mobilize and move forces.

Strategically, attacking Chinese cities to destroy civilian industry and infrastructure would cause the immediate dispersion of the leadership away from such areas and give propaganda value for the Communists to galvanize the support of Chinese civilians.

Since the Soviets were not expected to intervene with their few primitive atomic weapons on China or North Korea's behalf, the threat of a possible nuclear exchange was unimportant in the decision not to deploy atomic bombs; their use offered little operational advantage and would undesirably lower the "threshold" for using atomic weapons against non-nuclear states in future conflicts.

When Eisenhower succeeded Truman in early 1953, he was similarly cautious about using nuclear weapons in Korea. The administration prepared contingency plans to use them against China, but like Truman, the new president feared that doing so would result in Soviet attacks on Japan.

The war ended as it began, without U.S. nuclear weapons deployed near battle.

CHAPTER 33

War Crimes

Civilian deaths and massacres

South Korean soldiers walk among the bodies of political prisoners executed near Daejon, July 1950

Civilians killed during a night battle near Yongsan, August 1950

There were numerous atrocities and massacres of civilians throughout the Korean War committed by both sides, starting in the war's first days. On 28 June 1950, North Korean troops committed the Seoul National University Hospital massacre.

On the same day, South Korean President Syngman Rhee ordered the Bodo League massacre, beginning mass killings of suspected leftist sympathizers and their families by South Korean officials and right-wing groups.

Estimates of those killed during the Bodo League massacre range from at least 60,000–110,000, Kim Dong-choo, to 200,000, Park Myunglim.

The British protested to their allies about later South Korean mass executions and saved some citizens.

In 2005–2010, a South Korean Truth and Reconciliation Commission investigated atrocities and other human rights violations through much of the 20th century, from the Japanese colonial period through the Korean War and beyond.

It excavated some mass graves from the Bodo League massacres and confirmed the general outlines of those political executions.

Of the Korean War-era massacres the commission was petitioned to investigate, 82% were perpetrated by South Korean forces, with 18% perpetrated by North Korean forces.

The commission also received petitions alleging more than 200 large-scale killings of South Korean civilians by the U.S. military during the war, mostly air attacks.

It confirmed several such cases, including refugees crowded into a cave attacked with napalm bombs, which survivors said killed 360 people, and an air attack that killed 197 refugees gathered in a field in the far south.

It recommended South Korea seek reparations from the United States, but in 2010, a reorganized commission under a new, conservative government concluded that most U.S. mass killings resulted from "military necessity", while in a small number of cases, they concluded, the U.S. military had acted with "low levels of unlawfulness", but the commission recommended against seeking reparations.

In the most notorious U.S. massacre, investigated separately, not by the commission, American troops killed an estimated 250–300 refugees, mostly women and children, at No Gun Ri in central South Korea, 26–29 July 1950.

U.S. commanders, fearing enemy infiltrators among refugee columns, had adopted a policy of stopping civilian groups approaching U.S. lines, including by gunfire.

After years of rejecting survivors' accounts, the U.S. Army investigated and in 2001 acknowledged the No Gun Ri killings, but claimed they were not ordered and "not a deliberate killing".

South Korean officials, after a parallel investigation, said they believed there were orders to shoot. The survivors' representatives denounced what they described as a U.S. "whitewash".

The U.S. bombing of North Korea has been condemned as a war crime by some authors because it often included bombing civilian targets and caused many civilians casualties.

According to Bruce Cummings, "What hardly any Americans know or remember is that we carpet-bombed the north for three years with next to no concern for civilian casualties."

Author Blaine Harden has called the bombing campaign a "major war crime" and described it as "long, leisurely and merciless". He says it's "perhaps the most forgotten part of a forgotten war".

CHAPTER 34

Prisoners of War (POWs)

North Korean and Chinese prisoners of war in a camp at Pusan in April 1951

Chinese POWs

Chinese sources claim at Geoje prison camp on Geoje Island, Chinese POWs experienced anti-Communist lecturing and missionary work from secret agents from the U.S. and Taiwan in No. 71, 72 and 86 camps.

Pro-Communist POWs experienced torture, cutting off limbs, or were executed in public.

Being forced to write confession letters and receiving tattoos of an anti-Communism slogan and Flag of the Republic of China were also commonly seen in case any wanted to go back to mainland China.

Pro-Communist POWs who could not endure the torture formed an underground group to fight the pro-Nationalist POWs secretly by assassination, which led to the Geoje uprising.

The rebellion captured Francis Dodd and was suppressed by the 187th Infantry Regiment.

In the end, 14,235 Chinese POWs went to Taiwan and fewer than 6,000 POWs returned to mainland China.

Those who went to Taiwan are called "righteous men" and experienced brainwashing again and were sent to the army or were arrested; while the survivors who returned to mainland China were welcomed as a "hero" first, but experienced anti-brainwashing, strict interrogation, and house arrest eventually, after the tattoos were discovered.

After 1988, the Taiwanese government allowed POWs to go back to mainland China and helped remove anti-Communist tattoos; while the mainland Chinese government started to allow mainland Chinese prisoners of war to return from Taiwan.

UN Command POWs

The United States reported that North Korea mistreated prisoners of war: soldiers were beaten, starved, put to forced labor, marched to death, and summarily executed.

The KPA killed POWs at the battles for Hill 312, Hill 303, the Pusan Perimeter, Daejeon and Sunchon; these massacres were discovered afterwards by the UN forces.

Later, a U.S. Congress war crimes investigation, the United States Senate Subcommittee on Korean War Atrocities of the Permanent Subcommittee of the Investigations of the Committee on Government Operations, reported that "two-thirds of all American prisoners of war in Korea died as a result of war crimes".

Although the Chinese rarely executed prisoners like their North Korean counterparts, mass starvation and diseases swept through the Chinese-run POW camps during the winter of 1950–51. About 43 percent of U.S. POWs died during this period.

The Chinese defended their actions by stating that all Chinese soldiers during this period were suffering mass starvation and diseases due to logistical difficulties.

The UN POWs said that most of the Chinese camps were located near the easily supplied Sino-Korean border and that the Chinese withheld food to force the prisoners to accept the communism indoctrination programs.

According to Chinese reports, over a thousand U.S. POWs died by the end of June 1951, while a dozen British POWs died, and all Turkish POWs survived.

According to Hastings, wounded U.S. POWs died for lack of medical attention and were fed a diet of corn and millet "devoid of vegetables, almost barren of proteins, minerals, or vitamins" with only 1/3 the calories of their usual diet.

Especially in early 1951, thousands of prisoners lost the will to live and "declined to eat the mess of sorghum and rice they were provided".

CHAPTER 35

Two men without shirts on sit surrounded by soldiers

Two Hill 303 survivors after being rescued by U.S. units, 17 August 1950

The unpreparedness of U.S. POWs to resist heavy Communist indoctrination during the Korean War led to the Code of the United States Fighting Force which governs how U.S. military personnel in combat should act when they must "evade capture, resist while a prisoner or escape from the enemy".

North Korea may have detained up to 50,000 South Korean POWs after the ceasefire.

Over 88,000 South Korean soldiers were missing, and the KPA claimed they captured 70,000 South Koreans.

However, when ceasefire negotiations began in 1951, the KPA reported they held only 8,000 South Koreans.

The UN Command protested the discrepancies and alleged that the KPA were forcing South Korean POWs to join the KPA.

The KPA denied such allegations. They claimed their POW rosters were small because many POWs were killed in UN air raids and that they had released ROK soldiers at the front. They insisted only volunteers were allowed to serve in the KPA.

By early 1952, UN negotiators gave up trying to get back the missing South Koreans. The POW exchange proceeded without access to South Korean POWs who were not on the PVA/KPA rosters.

North Korea continued to claim that any South Korean POW who stayed in the North did so voluntarily. However, since 1994, South Korean POWs have been escaping North Korea on their own after decades of captivity.

As of 2010, the South Korean Ministry of Unification reported that 79 ROK POWs escaped the North. The South Korean government estimates 500 South Korean POWs continue to be detained in North Korea.

The escaped POWs have testified about their treatment and written memoirs about their lives in North Korea.

They report they were not told about the POW exchange procedures and were assigned to work in mines in the remote northeastern regions near the Chinese and Russian border.

Declassified Soviet Foreign Ministry documents corroborate such testimony.

In 1997, the Geoje POW Camp in South Korea was turned into a memorial.

Starvation

In December 1950, the South Korean National Defense Corps was founded; the soldiers were 406,000 drafted citizens.

In the winter of 1951, 50,000 to 90,000 South Korean National Defense Corps soldiers starved to death while marching southward under the PVA offensive when their commanding officers embezzled funds earmarked for their food.

Although his political allies certainly profited from corruption, it remains controversial if Syngman Rhee was personally involved in or benefited from the corruption.

CHAPTER 36

Recreation

United Service Organizations

Bob Hope entertained X Corps in Korea on 26 October 1950

In 1950, Secretary of Defense George C. Marshall and Secretary of the Navy Francis P. Matthews called on the United Service Organizations, USO, which was disbanded by 1947 to provide support for U.S. servicemen.

By the end of the war, more than 113,000 USO volunteers from the U.S. were working at the home front and abroad.

Many stars came to Korea to give their performances. Throughout the Korean War, comfort stations, brothels, were operated by South Korean officials for UN soldiers despite prostitution being ostensibly illegal.

CHAPTER 37

Aftermath

Aftermath of the Korean War

Postwar recovery was different in the two Koreas. South Korea, which started from a far lower industrial base than North Korea, the latter contained 80% of Korea's heavy industry in 1945, stagnated in the first postwar decade. In 1953, South Korea and the United States signed a Mutual Defense Treaty.

In 1960, the April Revolution occurred, and students joined an anti-Syngman Rhee demonstration; 142 were killed by police; in consequence, Syngman Rhee resigned and left for exile in the United States.

Park Chung Hee's May 16 coup enable social stability. From 1965 to 1973, South Korea dispatched troops to South Vietnam and received $235,560,000 in allowance and military procurement from the United States.

GNP increased fivefold during the Vietnam War. South Korea industrialized and modernized. South Korea had one of the world's fastest-growing economies from the early 1960s to the mid-1990s. In 1957, South Korea had a lower per capita GDP than Ghana, and by 2010, it was a developed country and ranked thirteenth in the world Ghana was 86th.

As a result of the war, "North Korea had been virtually destroyed as an industrial society". After the armistice, Kim Il Sung requested Soviet economic and industrial assistance. In September 1953, the Soviet government agreed to "cancel or postpone repayment for all… outstanding debts" and promised to grant North Korea one billion rubles in monetary aid, industrial equipment, and consumer goods.

Eastern European members of the Soviet Bloc also contributed with "logistical support, technical aid, and medical supplies". China canceled North Korea's war debts, provided 800 million yuan, promised trade cooperation, and sent in thousands of troops to rebuild damaged infrastructure. Contemporary North Korea remains underdeveloped.

North Korea has continued to be a totalitarian dictatorship since the end of the war, with an elaborate cult of personality around the Kim dynasty.

The means of production are owned by the state through state-run enterprises and collectivized farms. Most services, such as healthcare, education, housing, and food production, are subsidized or state funded.

Estimates based on the most recent North Korean census suggest that 240,000 to 420,000 people died because of the 1990s North Korean famine and that there were 600,000 to 850,000 unnatural deaths in North Korea from 1993 to 2008.

A study by South Korean anthropologists of North Korean children who had defected to China found that 18-year-old males were 13 cm (5 in) shorter than South Koreans their age because of malnutrition.

CHAPTER 38

The Korean Peninsula at night, shown in a 2012 composite photograph from NASA

Present-day North Korea follows Songun, or "military-first" policy. It is the country with the highest number of military and paramilitary personnel, with a total of 7,769,000 active, reserve, and paramilitary personnel, or approximately 30% of its population.

Its active-duty army of 1.28 million is the fourth largest in the world, after China, the United States and India, consisting of 4.9% of its population. North Korea possesses nuclear weapons.

A 2014 UN inquiry into abuses of human rights in North Korea concluded that, "the gravity, scale and nature of these violations reveal a state that does not have any parallel in the contemporary world," with Amnesty International and Human Rights Watch holding similar views.

South Korean anti-Americanism after the war was fueled by the presence and behavior of U.S. military personnel (USFK) and U.S. support for Park's authoritarian regime, a fact still evident during the country's democratic transition in the 1980s.

However, anti-Americanism has declined significantly in South Korea in recent years, from 46% favorable in 2003 to 74% favorable in 2011, making South Korea one of the most pro-U.S. countries in the world.

Many mixed-race "GI babies", offspring of U.S. and other UN soldiers and Korean women, were filling up the country's orphanages.

Because Korean traditional society places significant weight on paternal family ties, bloodlines, and purity of race, children of mixed race or those without fathers are not easily accepted in South Korean society.

International adoption of Korean children began in 1954.

The U.S. Immigration Act of 1952 legalized the naturalization of non-Blacks and non-Whites as U.S. citizens and made possible the entry of military spouses and children from South Korea after the Korean War.

With the passage of the Immigration Act of 1965, which substantially changed U.S. immigration policy toward non-Europeans, Koreans became one of the fastest-growing Asian groups in the United States.

Mao Zedong's decision to take on the United States in the Korean War was a direct attempt to confront what the Communist bloc viewed as the strongest anti-Communist power in the world, undertaken at a time when the Chinese Communist regime was still consolidating its own power after winning the Chinese Civil War.

Mao supported intervention not to save North Korea, but because he believed that a military conflict with the U.S. was inevitable after the U.S. entered the war, and to appease the Soviet Union to secure military dispensation and achieve Mao's goal of making China a major world military power.

Mao was equally ambitious in improving his own prestige inside the communist international community by demonstrating that his Marxist concerns were international. In his later years, Mao believed that Stalin only gained a positive opinion of him after China's entrance into the Korean War.

Inside mainland China, the war improved the long-term prestige of Mao, Zhou, and Peng, allowing the Chinese Communist Party to increase its legitimacy while weakening anti-Communist dissent.

CHAPTER 39

North Koreans touring the Museum of American War Atrocities in 2009.

The Chinese government has encouraged the viewpoint that the war was initiated by the United States and South Korea, though Comintern documents have shown that Mao sought approval from Joseph Stalin to enter the war.

In Chinese media, the Chinese war effort is considered as an example of China's engaging the strongest power in the world with an underequipped army, forcing it to retreat, and fighting it to a military stalemate.

These successes were contrasted with China's historical humiliations by Japan and by Western powers over the previous hundred years, highlighting the abilities of the PLA and the Chinese Communist Party.

The most significant negative long-term consequence of the war for China was that it led the United States to guarantee the safety of Chiang Kaishek's regime in Taiwan, effectively ensuring that Taiwan would remain outside of PRC control through the present day.

Mao had also discovered the usefulness of large-scale mass movements in the war while implementing them among most of his ruling measures over PRC.

Finally, anti-U.S. sentiments, which were already a significant factor during the Chinese Civil War, were ingrained into Chinese culture during the Communist propaganda campaigns of the Korean War.

The Korean War affected other participant combatants. Turkey, for example, entered NATO in 1952, and the foundation was laid for bilateral diplomatic and trade relations with South Korea.

CHAPTER 40

The Forgotten Heroes of a Forgotten War

This week, dozens of aging combat veterans made their way to Washington D.C. Early on the morning of Wednesday, April 13, they completed an almost mandatory circuit taking them from the Tomb of the Unknown Soldier in Arlington National Cemetery to the World War II and Korean War memorials in the National Mall.

They took part in wreath laying ceremonies at these monuments—an act of remembrance and respect for those fallen in combat and the ones still missing. Many of the veterans couldn't contain their tears as the bugle played "Taps".

Who knows where the melody transported them? Did they remember battles fought? Friends lost? The terror of war? The pride they felt for their service. The price they paid in their youth?

This scene is a common occurrence at these sites. Veterans from the many wars this country has fought find their way to these monuments triggering memories of days long gone and reopening unhealed, invisible wounds.

This time, most of these veterans were Puerto Ricans who fought in the Korean War with the 65th U.S. Army Infantry Regiment, also known as "el sesenta y cinco de infantería." Regardless of where they came from, they were all "Borinqueneers."

The wreath laying ceremonies were only the beginning of a long day which ended on a high note at Emancipation Hall in the Capitol building.

The Borinqueneers were there to witness the unveiling of the Congressional Gold Medal awarded to the regiment on June 10, 2014. Earning this medal was no small feat. Since the American Revolution, Congress has commissioned gold medals as its highest expression of national appreciation for distinguished achievements and contributions.

Since George Washington received it in 1776, only 158 individuals and entities have been awarded the medal to date. The 65th is the first unit to receive it for service during the Korean War. They join Roberto Clemente, who earned it posthumously, as the only Puerto Rican or Latino CGM recipients.

Think about this for a second; the medal represents the highest expression of national appreciation for distinguished achievements and contributions. What were these men's contributions and achievements? Why do we honor them today for service performed during a conflict known as the "Forgotten War" more than sixty years ago?

The answers lie in these men's service that many times required them to fight on two fronts. They fought relentless North Korean and Chinese soldiers in fierce combat in the hills, valleys, villages, and cities of Korea.

They also fought discrimination, often coming from the men supposed to be leading them.

The role of the Puerto Rican soldiers in Korea was as important at the Navajo Code Talkers', the Tuskegee Airmen's, or the Nissei Regiment's role in WWII in destroying racial prejudices holding that that non-Whites were inferior men, unfit for combat, and undeserving of equality and self-determination and self-rule.

The 65th Infantry originated as Puerto Rican outfit in the form of the Battalion of Porto Rican Volunteers, May 20, 1899, in the aftermath of the Spanish-American War of 1898.

They were regarded as colonial troops, part of the first "American Colonial Army." In 1908, and by then a regiment, the unit officially became part of the U.S. Army. It came to be known as the Porto Rican Regiment. During WWI the regiment was sent to the Canal Zone in Panama- far from the European battlefields.

In 1920, the unit's name changed from the Porto Rican Regiment to the 65th Infantry Regiment, United States Army.

While African American troops saw their role extended during WWII, greatly in part to Black leaders' involvement in demanding access to combat positions and officers commissions, Puerto Rican units were kept from any assignment that may involve combat.

The 65th served in North Africa and Europe during World War II, but not as first-line troops. Military authorities, reflecting the racial prejudice of the time, kept the regiment far from the front.

The military followed a policy of racial segregation in which combat roles, with a few exceptions, were reserved for White troops. The military's institutional racism had unintended consequences.

As the 65th was kept from combat it underwent all kinds of training and its men and officers dutifully prepared for war. Non-combat assignments meant that the Borinqueneers suffered very few casualties throughout the war. By WWII's end the 65th was a superbly trained and well-disciplined combat regiment.

The story of the 65th could've ended right after WWII as the U.S. military rapidly demobilized the 12 million Americans in uniform. There was no reason to keep the "Rum & Coke" outfit around, as the 65th was referred to in derision.

The unit was gradually demobilized. However, on June 24, 1950, war broke out in Korea. We know what happened next.

An unprepared U.S. military had to scrap the bottom of the barrel to find men and units ready for combat. In Puerto Rico, the National Guard was activated, and the 65th was mobilized and ordered to Korea.

The Borinqueneers were going to war as first-line combat troops, as part of the Army's 3rd Infantry Division.

On October 12, 1950, Puerto Ricans learned that the 65th was fighting in Korea. The island's newspapers were full of stories and pictures of the soldiers and the ceremonies held before their departure.

Island-wide, the people of Puerto Rico joined to support the 65th throughout the war. Governor Luis Muñoz Marín often referred to the men of the 65th in his speeches. The crest of the 65th was displayed in public buses and train cars.

Plazas and avenues were named to honor the regiment. Returning soldiers, especially the wounded, were received as heroes and treated to public receptions by government officials.

Muñoz Marín himself attended the burials of the fallen and sent his recorded speeches to the troops in Korea.

In those early days of the war, there was not a day in which the island's press failed to write about the Puerto Rican soldiers, and what their actions meant for Puerto Rico.

During the war, the 65th became a national icon on the island and among the growing Puerto Rican communities in the mainland.

The island-based press and elected officials linked fighting in Korea with decolonization and the commonwealth formula.

Moreover, lengthy press editorials and the governor referred to the 65th as a catalyst for achieving full manhood, forging a modern Puerto Rican, and a modern Puerto Rico.

Among the growing Puerto Rican colonial in New York the actions of the Borinqueneers and Puerto Ricans were used in what we call nowadays "policies of respectability."

At a time in which mainstream media and social sciences talked openly about the "Puerto Rican problem" as more and more Puerto Ricans migrated to the continental U.S., local publications highlighted the Borinqueneers' heroics to counter the community's detractors.

The majority of the 61,000 Puerto Ricans who fought in the Korean War came from the island. Many served with the 65th. The vast majority were volunteers who several times completed the island's monthly recruiting quota.

The chance that they may be sent to the 65th motivated thousands of Puerto Ricans to volunteer for service both in the mainland and on the island. Throughout the conflict 3,540 Puerto Ricans became casualties of war, of whom 747 were killed in action.

The odyssey of these men helped established a bridge, and air route between New York and the island, and it helped to ensure the survival of Puerto Rican communities in the eastern seaboard.

Recruits and volunteers came mostly from the island. They were transported in cargo ships from Puerto Rico through the Panama Canal and from there to Korea, sometimes stopping in Hawaii and/or Japan before landing in Korea.

Their return was different, especially for the wounded and repatriated prisoners of war POW.

As any other American soldiers, gravely wounded Puerto Rican would be evacuated from Korea and find their way to the continental United States. After a stay in Walter Reed Medical Hospital, most of these men would be returned to Puerto Rico.

Their voyage was one that millions of Puerto Ricans after them would undertake. They would fly from Baltimore to LaGuardia Airport in New York where they would stay for a day or two.

Once in New York, the returning soldiers would participate in parades in el Bronx and in Harlem. The city's mayor would usually meet them along with city and community leaders and offer the key to the city to them.

Their heroics were highlighted in articles next to news on the persecution of Puerto Ricans from Brooklyn to el Bronx. Moreover, they would return to the island aboard recently refurbished Eastern Airlines planes.

This firm flew many soldiers, free of charge, to the island. The airline's advertisement for the new non-stop flights from San Juan to New York dotted the Puerto Rican and Latino press in the city.

The actions of the Borinqueneers during the first half of the war elevated them to iconic status- living proof of what Puerto Ricans could do when given the opportunity, showing they were second to none, inferior to no one.

Then, tragedy struck. The replacement of highly trained, combat-hardened troops with poorly trained, yet enthusiastic, recruits who spoke little English; an acute dearth of bilingual sergeants, the backbone of the American military; and new Continental officers that did not speak Spanish, some of whom openly showed their despised for Puerto Rican soldiers, led to tragic events during the battles of Outpost Kelly and Jackson Heights in the autumn of 1952.

The back-to-back disasters were followed by a series of mass court martial in which eighty-seven enlisted men and one Puerto Rican officer received sentences ranging from six months to ten years, and total forfeiture of wages and dishonorable discharges for charges varying from willful disobedience of a superior officer to cowardice before the enemy.

In 1953, the Secretary of the Army reviewed the cases and remitted the unexecuted portions of the sentences of all but four of the accused. The soldiers who had their sentences remitted were returned to duty.

On March 4, 1953, an Army spokesman announced that the Army had decided to integrate the 65th Infantry with Continental troops, and to redistribute to other units the excess Puerto Rican troops.

The 65th would no longer be a Puerto Rican unit. Despite the soldiers' objections the regiment was quickly integrated as planned.

In 1954, the 65th Infantry returned to Puerto Rico and was reconstituted as an all-Puerto Rican formation. The island had its regiment back, but not for long. It was deactivated in 1956.

Colonel César Cordero, who had led the 65th during the tragic battle for Outpost Kelly, led a campaign that culminated with the reactivation and transfer of the 65th from the Army to the Puerto Rico National Guard in 1959.

Unlike its participation during the war, this event received scant publicity and soon the Borinqueneers and their epic ordeal faded into a distant and distorted memory, the forgotten heroes of a forgotten war.

On June 13, 2016, el setenta y Cinco was awarded the highest accolade Congress can give. The Borinqueneers went from forgotten soldiers who had to face both the enemy and discrimination, to heroes earning praise from the leaders of Congress and the military.

In his closing speech, Speaker of the House Paul Ryan commented that "it takes a certain caliber of men" to fight for a country "that discriminates against you." Dr. Barry Black, the Chaplain of the United States Senate asked God for forgiveness for segregating the Puerto Rican soldiers and for being slow in recognizing their sacrifice and heroism. Every speaker had honest and overdue praise for these men.

It has always puzzled me that the efforts to recover the history of the Borinqueneers and to restore their record came mostly from members of the Puerto Rican migration.

Today, I understood why. As the United States Army Band played "En mi Viejo San Juan," the unofficial anthem of a Diaspora dreaming of a return to Borinquen the ceremony attendees, veterans, their relatives, and new generations of Puerto Rican soldiers, joined and sang along the band. Many wept.

The faces of the members of Congress present made me think that they had never seen such a display of national pride.

It did not matter where these soldiers were sent, what task they were asked to perform, they never stopped being Borinqueneers and carrying a bit of Puerto Rico everywhere they went.

Several soldiers, and, while proud of their service and of the recognition they were receiving, could not help but to be humble and simply state that they were just doing their duty. They did more than that.

During the Korean War they carried a heavy burden as the hopes for a new Puerto Rico and winning acceptance for the growing Diaspora rested largely on their performance in combat. They did their best, many times against all odds, even if it was not always recognized.

Their numbers are shrinking. Roughly a thousand of them remain. Eventually, all will be gone but not forgotten, they will not fade away.

Let's take over their burden and make sure that their sacrifices were not in vain, let's make sure that their legacy survives and continues to inspire new generations of Puerto Ricans.

CHAPTER 41

Puerto Ricans Missing in action in the Korean War

The United States Department of Defense has estimated that approximately 61,000 Puerto Ricans served in the military during the Korean War, most of them volunteers.

A total of 122 Puerto Rican soldiers were among the 8,200 people listed as missing in action (MIA). According to the Defense POW/MIA Accounting Agency, there are 167 who are unaccounted for.

This list does not include non-Puerto Ricans who served in the 65th Infantry, nor those who were "POW", Prisoners of War, or "KIA", Killed in Action. Nor does the total of this list include people of Puerto Rican descent who were born in the mainland of the United States.

Spain officially ceded Puerto Rico to the United States under the terms of the 1898 Treaty of Paris which concluded the Spanish American War.

It is a United States territory and upon the outbreak of World War I, the Congress enacted the Jones–Shafroth Act, which gave Puerto Ricans American citizenship with certain limitations, for example, Puerto Ricans are not allowed to vote in presidential elections.

Thousands of Puerto Ricans participated in these conflicts. Many lived and returned to their homeland, others either died or have been listed as missing in action.

The term "MIA" dates from 1946 and refers to a member of the armed services who is reported missing following a combat mission and whose status as to injury, capture, or death is unknown.

The missing combatant must not have been otherwise accounted for as either killed in action or a prisoner of war.

The Korean War was one of two major conflicts which accounted for the most Puerto Ricans missing in action, the other being the Vietnam War.

PFC Ramón Núñez-Juárez

According to the online archive "All POW-MIA Korean War Casualties," the total number of Puerto Rican casualties in the Korean War was 732. Out of the more than 700 casualties suffered in the war, a total of 122 Puerto Rican men were listed as Missing in Action.

It was during the Korean War that Puerto Ricans suffered the most casualties as members of an all-Hispanic volunteer unit: the 65th Infantry Regiment.

One of the problems the unit faced was the language difference; the common foot soldier spoke only Spanish, while the commanding officers were mostly English-speaking.

In September 1952, the 65th Infantry was holding onto a hill known as "Outpost Kelly" until the People's Volunteer Army which had joined the North Koreans, overran the position.

This became known as the Battle for Outpost Kelly. Twice, the 65th Regiment was overwhelmed by Chinese artillery and driven off. The Battle of Outpost Kelly accounted for 73 of the men missing in action from the total of 122.

Out of the 73 MIAs suffered by the regiment in the month of September, 50 of them occurred on the same day: September 18.

According to the Defense POW/MIA Accounting Agency seven Puerto Ricans who were members of the United States Marine Corps, except for PFC Ramón Núñez-Juárez and PFC Manuel Perez-Pizarro who were Killed in Action.

PFC Enrique Romero-Nieves and PFC Ramón Núñez-Juárez were awarded the Navy Cross, the second highest medal after the Medal of Honor that can be awarded by the Department of the Navy.

Ramón Núñez-Juárez, who was listed as MIA, was posthumously awarded the medal. Núñez-Juárez's remains have never been recovered and a symbolic burial with full military honors was held on October 25, 1970.

There is a headstone with his name inscribed above an empty grave in the Puerto Rico National Cemetery, located in Bayamon, Puerto Rico.

His name and that of the others are inscribed in El Monumento de la Recordación, a monument dedicated to the Puerto Ricans who have fallen in combat, located in San Juan, Puerto Rico.

Puerto Ricans missing in action

The following is a list with the names, ranks and the date in which 122 Puerto Ricans were listed as missing in action in the Korean War.

All these men served within the ranks of the United States Army except for Ramón Núñez-Juárez and Francisco González Matías, who served in the United States Marine Corps.

Isaac Acevedo	Corporal	September 18, 1952
Héctor Alfaro Alfaro	Private	September 24, 1952
Hugo Álvarez	Corporal	June 5, 1951
Luis Amaro García	Private first-class	September 18, 1952
Euripides Amy-Colon	Private first-class	February 6, 1952
Lopus Andino Fonseca	Private	September 24, 1952
Jorge Berríos Santiago	Private	September 24, 1952
Julio Bonilla Vega	Private	September 18, 1952
José Burset Meléndez	Private	September 24, 1952
A Caballero Moreno	Private first-class	April 1953

Juan Calderón Osorio	Private first-class	September 18, 1952
A Calimano Texidor	Private	September 18, 1952
Benigno Caraballo	Private	December 11, 1951
Juan Caramot Ortiz	Private	September 24, 1952
Miguel Cartagena Colón	Private	Unknown
Manuel Colon Aponte	Private first-class	September 18, 1952
Concepción Colón	Private	July 31, 1952
Luis Colón Negrón	Private	September 24, 1952
José Concepción López	Private first-class	September 18, 1952
James W. Connor	Captain	December 1, 1950
Zenon Cordero Cajigas	Private	September 24, 1952
Ángel Cortés Ostolaza	Private	September 24, 1952
Francisco Cosme Báez	Private first-class	September 18, 1952
Jesús Cruz Beltrán	Private first-class	September 18, 1952
José Cruz Carrero	Private first-class	September 18, 1952
Roberto Cruz Espinoza	Private	June 4, 1951
Nicolás Cruz Pérez	Corporal	June 10, 1953
Jesús Cruz Ramos	Private first-class	June 9, 1953
Pablo Cruz Rosas	Private first-class	November 25, 1952
Ángel Cruz Sánchez	Private first-class	September 10, 1952
Carlos Dávila Rivera	Private	September 14, 1952
Wenceslao Delgado Ubiles	Private	October 19, 1952
Luis Díaz Acevedo	Private	September 18, 1952
Demetrio Díaz Algarín	Private	September 18, 1952
Fernando Díaz Colón	Private	September 18, 1952
Rafael Díaz Coto	Private	September 18, 1952
Saúl Droz Cartagena	Private first-class	December 15, 1952
Carlos D. Feliciano	Private	September 18, 1952
Julio Feliciano Nieves	Private	September 18, 1952
Bienvenido Feliciano Otero	Private	September 18, 1952
Luis Figueroa Barbosa	Private	September 18, 1952
Julio Flores Navarro	Private	October 15, 1952
Ismael García Clara	Private	September 18, 1952

Cándido García Rosado	Private first-class	September 25, 1952
Manuel González Bernard	Private	September 18, 1952
Israel González Nazario	Private	July 17, 1952
Juan E. González Ortiz	Private	September 18, 1952
Porfirio González Renta	Private	September 18, 1952
Ángel González Rosario	Private	September 18, 1952
Israel González Saez	Private	September 18, 1952
Santos González	Private	September 18, 1952
Isidro Hernández Dones	Corporal	September 21, 1952
Luis Hernández Rodríguez	Private	September 18, 1952
Benjamín Hernández Torres	Private first-class	August 12, 1952
O. Irizarry Gerena	Private	December 16, 1951
A. Jiménez Olivencia	Corporal	September 18, 1952
Miguel Jiménez Tosado	Private first-class	July 9, 1953
Maximian Lacsamana	Corporal	December 3, 1950
Jaime Laugier	Corporal	February 16, 1952
Luis López Cronoz	Private	September 18, 1952
Herminio Luciano Rodriguez	Private first-class	December 9, 1952
Israel Malaret Juarbe	Sergeant first class	December 10, 1952
Ramón Marquez De León	Private first-class	October 27, 1952
Luis Martínez Hernández	Private	September 18, 1952
Ramon Martínez Landrón	Private	September 21, 1952
Luis Martínez	Private	November 6, 1952
Pedro Martínez Otero	Corporal	September 18, 1952
Francisco Matos González	Private first-class	September 18, 1952
Alberto Meléndez Meléndez	Private first-class	October 23, 1952
Marcial Meléndez Negrón	Corporal	September 24, 1952
Luis Méndez Hernández	Corporal	July 19, 1952
Salomé Mercado Hernández	Private first-class	September 18, 1952
Carlos Miranda Cotto	Private first class	September 18, 1952
Roberto Molina García	Private first-class	September 21, 1952
Maximino Molina Gerena	Corporal	February 6, 1952
Sixto Montañez Franco	Private first-class	September 18, 1952

Alfredo Morales Reyes	Corporal	August 14, 1952
Nelson Moreno Rosa	Corporal	September 18, 1952
Ramón Murga Amador	Private first-class	September 18, 1952
José A. Napoleón Escudero	Private	September 18, 1952
Jorge Negrón Martínez	Private first-class	September 18, 1952
José Negrón Ortiz	Corporal	September 18, 1952
Arcadio Nieves Larry	Corporal	September 24, 1952
Ramón Núñez-Juárez	Private first-class	September 8, 1952
Bartolomé Pacheco	Private	January 8, 1952
Juan Peña Andújar	Private first-class	September 18, 1952
Miguel Pérez	Private first-class	January 8, 1952
Pedro Pérez Pérez	Private first-class	August 12, 1952
Efraín Pérez Rodríguez	Corporal	July 20, 1952
Luis Pérez Villegas	Private	September 18, 1952
Nicolás Pizarro Matos	Private first-class	September 18, 1952
Pedro Pomales Pomales	Private	September 21, 1952
Pedro Angel Quiñones Velez	Corporal	September 24, 1952
Marino Quirindongo	Private	December 16, 1951
Marcos Reyes Rodríguez	Private	October 27, 1952
William Reyes	Private	June 5, 1951
Juan Rivera Carrillo	Private first-class	October 28, 1952
Roberto Rivera Claudio	Private	October 1952
Gilberto Rivera Cruz	Private first- class	September 18, 1952
Israel Rivera Galarza	Private first-class	September 18, 1952
Luis P. Rivera	Private first-class	September 26, 1952
Raul Rivera Rodríguez	Private first-class	September 18, 1952
Rubén Rivera	Private	September 24, 1952
Enrique Rodríguez	Private	July 8, 1953
Alberto Rodríguez Lozada	Sergeant first -class	June 4, 1951
Pedro A. Rodríguez	Private first-class	January 11, 1952
Juan Rojas Reyes	Private first-class	September20, 1952
Ramón Roque Peña	Private first-class	October 16, 1952
José Rosado Bravo	Private first-class	September 18, 1952

Francisco Rosario Meléndez	Private first-class	September 18, 1952
Ángel Salgado Torres	Private	January 8, 1952
Ángel S. Sanabria	Private first-class	January 28, 1952
Rafael Sánchez López	Private first-class	September 18, 1952
Angel L. Santiago	Private	June 3, 1951
José Santiago Ortiz	Private first-class	October 14, 1952
Ramón Santiago Rosario	Sergeant	February 6, 1952
Norberto Santos Rivero	Corporal	June 4, 1951
Nicolás Santos Rosario	Private first-class	December 11, 1951
José Torres Cabán	First lieutenant	September 29, 1950
Jorge Torres Green	Private	July 19, 1952
Samuel Torres Rodríguez	Private first-class	September 18, 1952
Jorge L. Vázquez	Sergeant	February 6, 1952
Luis Vélez Montes	Private first-class	September 18, 1952
Miguel Vélez Santiago	Private	December 23, 1951
Miguel A. Zayas	Private first-class	February 6, 1952

CHAPTER 42

Military History of Puerto Rico

The recorded military history of Puerto Rico encompasses the period from the 16th century, when Spanish conquistadores battled native Taínos in the rebellion of 1511, to the present employment of Puerto Ricans in the United States Armed Forces in the military campaigns in Afghanistan and Iraq.

Puerto Rico was part of the Spanish Empire for four centuries, during which the people of Puerto Rico defended themselves against invasions from the British, French, and Dutch.

Puerto Ricans fought alongside General Bernardo de Gálvez during the American Revolutionary War in the battles of Baton Rouge, Mobile, Pensacola and St. Louis. During the mid-19th century, Puerto Ricans residing in the United States fought in the American Civil War.

In the 1800s, the quest for Latin American independence from Spain spread to Puerto Rico, in the short-lived revolution known as the Grito de Lares and culminating with the Intentona de Yauco.

The island was invaded by the United States during the Spanish American War. After the war ended, Spain officially ceded the island to the United States under the terms established in the Treaty of Paris of 1898.

Puerto Rico became a United States territory, and the "Porto Rico Regiment" Puerto Rico's name was changed to Porto Rico was established on the island.

Upon the outbreak of World War I, the U.S. Congress approved the Jones–Shafroth Act, which extended United States citizenship the Puerto Rican House of Delegates rejected US citizenship with limitations upon Puerto Ricans and made them eligible for the military draft.

Since then, as citizens of the United States, Puerto Ricans have participated in every major United States military engagement.

During World War II, Puerto Ricans participated in the Pacific and Atlantic theaters, not only as combatants but also as commanders.

It was during this conflict that Puerto Rican nurses were allowed to participate as members of the WAACs. Four Puerto Ricans were awarded the Medal of Honor, the highest military honor in the United States, for their actions during the Korean War.

The members of Puerto Rico's 65th Infantry Regiment distinguished themselves in combat in the Korean War and were honored with the Congressional Gold Medal. During the Vietnam War five Puerto Ricans were awarded the Medal of Honor. Presently, Puerto Ricans continue to serve in the military of the United States.

Taíno rebellion of 1511

Christopher Columbus arrived in the island of Puerto Rico on November 19, 1493, during his second voyage to the so-called "New World".

The island was inhabited by the Arawak group of Indigenous peoples known as Taínos, who called the island "Borikén" or "Borinquen".

Columbus named the island San Juan Bautista in honor of Saint John the Baptist. The main port was named Puerto Rico (Rich Port) (eventually the island was renamed Puerto Rico and the port which was to evolve into the capital of the island was renamed San Juan). The conquistador Juan Ponce de León accompanied Columbus on this trip.

Agüeybaná, better known as
Agüeybaná II, The Brave

When Ponce de León arrived in Puerto Rico, he was well received by the Cacique Tribal chief Agüeybaná, The Great Sun, chieftain of the island Taino tribes.

Besides the conquistadors, some of the first colonists were farmers and miners in search of gold.

In 1508, Ponce de León became the first appointed governor of Puerto Rico, founding the first settlement of Caparra between the modern-day cities of Bayamón and San Juan.

After being named Governor, de León and the conquistadors forced the Taínos to work in the mines and to build fortifications; many Taínos died because of cruel treatment during their labor.

In 1510, upon Agüeybaná's death, his brother Agüeybaná, better known as Agüeybaná II, The Brave, and a group of Taínos led Diego Salcedo, a Spaniard, to a river and drowned him, proving to his people that the white men were not gods. Upon realizing this, Agüeybaná II led his people in the Taino rebellion of 1511, the first rebellion in the island against the better armed Spanish forces.

Guarini, cacique of Utuado, attacked the village of Sotomayor, present-day Aguada, and killed eighty of its inhabitants.

Cacique Guarini died during the attack which was considered a Taino victory.

After the Taino victory, the colonists formed a citizens' militia to defend themselves against the attacks. Juan Ponce de León and one of his top commanders, Diego de Salazar, led the Spaniards in a series of offensives which included a massacre of the Taino forces in the domain of Agüeybaná II.

The Spanish offensive culminated in the Battle of Yagüecas against Cacique Mabodomoca.

Agüeybaná II was shot and killed, ending the first recorded military action in Puerto Rico.

After the failed rebellion, the Taínos were forced to give up their customs and traditions by order of a Royal decree, approved by King Ferdinand II, which required that they adopt and practice the values, religion, and language of their conquerors.

CHAPTER 43

European powers fight over Puerto Rico

16th century

Puerto Rico was considered the "Key to the Caribbean" by the Spanish because of its location as a way station and port for Spanish vessels.

In 1540, with revenue from Mexican mines, the Spanish settlers began the construction of Fort San Felipe del Morro "the promontory" in San Juan. With the completion of the initial phase of the construction in 1589 El Morro became the island's main military fortification, guarded by professional soldiers.

The rest of Puerto Rico, which had been reorganized in 1580 as the Captaincy General of Puerto Rico, had to rely on only a handful of soldiers and the local volunteer militia to defend the island against militant and pirate attacks.

The main enemies of Spain at the time were the English and the Dutch. They, however, were not the only enemies that Spain faced in the Caribbean during this period.

On October 11, 1528, the French sacked and burned the settlement of San Germán during an attempt to capture the island, destroying many of the island's first settlements, including Guánica, Sotomayor, Daguao and Loiza, before the local militia forced them to retreat. The only settlement that remained was San Juan.

In 1585, war broke out between England and Spain, extending to Spanish and English territories in the Americas.

In November 1595, Sir Francis Drake and Sir John Hawkins attempted an unsuccessful invasion of San Juan.

On June 15, 1598, the English fleet, led by George Clifford, landed in Santurce, and held the island for 157 days. He was forced to abandon the island upon an outbreak of bacillary dysentery among his troops, losing 700 men to the outbreak.

On December 26, 1598, Alonso de Mercado, a military man was named to the Captaincy General of Puerto Rico by Spain and asked to punish anyone who had allowed the takeover, through negligence, malice, or cowardice.

17th century

The Dutch Republic was a world military and commercial power by 1625, competing in the Caribbean with the English. The Dutch wanted to establish a military stronghold in the area, and dispatched Captain Boudewijn Hendricksz also known as Boudoyno Henrico or Balduino Enrico to capture Puerto Rico.

On September 24, 1625, Enrico arrived at the coast of San Juan with 17 ships and 2,000 men. Enrico sent a message to the governor of Puerto Rico, Juan de Haro, ordering him to surrender the island. De Haro refused; he was an experienced military man and expected an attack in the section known as Boquerón.

He therefore had that area fortified. However, the Dutch took another route and landed in La Puntilla.

De Haro realized that an invasion was inevitable and ordered Captain Juan de Amézqueta and 300 men to defend the island from El Morro Castle and then had the city of San Juan evacuated.

He also had former governor Juan de Vargas organize an armed resistance in the interior of the island.

On September 25, Hendricksz attacked San Juan, besieging El Morro Castle and La Fortaleza, the Governor's Mansion. He invaded the capital city and set up his headquarters in La Fortaleza.

The Dutch were counterattacked by the civilian militia on land and by the cannons of the Spanish troops in El Morro Castle. The land battle left 60 Dutch soldiers dead and Hendricksz with a sword wound to his neck which he received from the hands of Amézqueta.

The Dutch ships at sea were boarded by Puerto Ricans, who defeated those aboard. After a long battle, the Spanish soldiers and volunteers of the city's militia were able to defend the city from the attack and save the island from an invasion.

On October 21, Hendricksz set La Fortaleza and the city ablaze. Captains Amézqueta and Andrés Botello decided to put a stop to the destruction and led 200 men in an attack against the enemy's front and rear guard. They drove Hendricksz and his men from their trenches and into the ocean in haste to reach their ships.

Hendricksz upon his retreat left behind him one of his largest ships, stranded, and over 400 dead.

He then tried to invade the island by attacking the town of Aguada. He was again defeated by the local militia and abandoned the idea of invading Puerto Rico.

In 1693, the Milicias Urbanas de Puerto Rico were organized in almost every town. Every native male, aged between 16 and 60, was obliged to serve in these companies, unless he had an official exemption on account of physical disability or family hardship.

Captain Miguel Henriquez

While Spain and England were in a power struggle in the New World, Puerto Rican privateering of English ships was encouraged by the Spanish Crown.

Captain Miguel Enríquez and Captain Roberto Cofresí, in the 19th century, were two of the most famous Puerto Rican privateers. In the first half of the 18th century, Henriquez, a shoemaker by occupation, decided to try his luck as a privateer.

He showed great valor in intercepting English merchant ships and other ships dedicated to contraband that were infesting the seas of Puerto Rico and the Atlantic Ocean in general.

Henriquez organized an expeditionary force which fought and defeated the English in the island of Vieques. He was received as a national hero when he returned the island of Vieques to the Spanish Empire and to the governorship of Puerto Rico.

In recognition of his service, the Spanish Crown awarded Henriquez the Medalla de Oro de la Real Efigie, "The Gold Medal of the Royal Effigy", named him "Captain of the Seas and War", and gave him a letter of marque and reprisal, thus granting him the privileges of privateer.

18th century
Armed conflicts with the British

The English continued their attacks against Spanish colonies in the Caribbean, taking minor islands including Vieques east of Puerto Rico.

On August 5, 1702, the city of Arecibo, on Puerto Rico's northern coast, was invaded by the British. Armed only with spears and machetes, under the command of Captain Antonio de los Reyes Correa, 30 militia members defended the city from the English, who were armed with muskets and swords.

The British were defeated, suffering 22 losses on land and 8 at sea. Reyes Correa was declared a national hero and was awarded the Medalla de Oro de la Real Efigie "Gold Medal of the Royal Image" and the title of "Captain of Infantry" by King Philip V.

Native-born Puerto Rican, criollos, had petitioned the Spanish Crown to serve in the regular Spanish army, resulting in the 1741 organization of the Regiment Fijo de Puerto Rico.

The Fijo served in the defense of Puerto Rico and other Spanish overseas possessions, performing in battles in Santo Domingo, other islands in the Caribbean, and South America, most notably in Venezuela.

However, Puerto Rican complaints that the Fijo was being used to suppress the revolution in Venezuela caused the Crown to bring the Fijo home and in 1815 it was mustered out of service.

In 1765, the Spanish Crown sent Field Marshal Alejandro O'Reilly to Puerto Rico to form an organized militia. O'Reilly, known as the "Father of the Puerto Rican Militia", oversaw training to bring fame and glory to the militia in future military engagements, nicknaming the civilian militia the "Disciplined Militia." O'Reilly was later appointed governor of colonial Louisiana in 1769 and became known as "Bloody O'Reilly."

CHAPTER 44

American Revolutionary War

Brigadier General Ramón de Castro

During the American Revolutionary War, Spain lent the rebelling colonists the use of its ports in Puerto Rico, through which flowed financial aid and arms for their cause.

An incident occurred in the coast of Mayagüez, in 1777, between two Continental Navy ships, the Eudawook and the Henry, and a Royal Navy warship, HMS Glasgow.

Both American ships were chased by the larger and more powerful Glasgow. The American colonial ships were close to the coast of Mayagüez; members of the Puerto Rican militia of that town, realizing that something was wrong, signaled for the ships to dock at the town's bay.

After the ships docked, the crews of both ships got off and some Mayagüezanos boarded and raised the Spanish flag on both ships. The commander of the Glasgow became aware of the situation and asked the island's governor, Jose Dufresne, to turn over the ships. Dufresne refused and ordered the British warship out of the Puerto Rican dock.

The governor of Louisiana, Bernardo de Gálvez, was named field marshal of the Spanish colonial army in North America.

In 1779, Galvez and his troops, composed of Puerto Ricans and people from other Spanish colonies, distracted the British from the revolution by capturing Pensacola, the capital of the British colony of West Florida and the cities of Baton Rouge, St. Louis and Mobile.

The Puerto Rican troops, under the leadership of Brigadier General Ramón de Castro,[26] helped defeat the British and Indian army of 2,500 soldiers and British warships in Pensacola.

Galvez and his multinational army also provided the Continental Army with guns, cloth, gunpowder, and medicine shipped from Cuba up the Mississippi River. General Ramón de Castro, who was Galvez's Aide-de-camp in the Mobile and Pensacola campaigns, became the appointed governor of Puerto Rico in 1795.

British attack Puerto Rico
Anglo-Spanish War (1796–1808) and
Battle of San Juan (1797)

On February 17, 1797, the governor of Puerto Rico Brigadier General Ramón de Castro, received news that Great Britain had invaded the island of Trinidad. Believing that Puerto Rico would be the next British objective he decided to put the local militia on alert and to prepare the island's forts against any military action.

On April 17, 1797, British ships under the command of Sir Ralph Abercromby approached the coastal town of Loíza, to the east of San Juan. On April 18, British and Hessian troops landed on Loíza's beach.

Under the command of de Castro, British ships were shot at by artillery from both El Morro and the San Gerónimo fortresses but were beyond reach.

After the invaders disembarked practically all fighting was land based with many skirmishes, field artillery and mortar fire exchanges between the San Gerónimo and San Antonio Bridge fortress and British emplacements in Condado to the East and El Olimpo hill in Miramar to the South.

The British tried to take the San Antonio, a key passage to the San Juan islet, and repeatedly bombarded the nearby San Gerónimo almost demolishing it.

At the Martín Peña Bridge, they were met by the likes of Sergeants José and Francisco Díaz and Colonel Rafael Conti who together with Lieutenant Lucas de Fuentes attacked the enemy with two cannons.

After fierce fighting by the Spanish forces and local militia, they were defeated in all attempts to advance into San Juan.

The invasion failed because Puerto Rican volunteers and Spanish troops fought back and defended the island in a manner described by a British lieutenant as of "astonishing bravery".

CHAPTER 45

"La Rogativa" folklore

The defense of San Juan served as the base for the legend of "La Rogativa". According to the popular Puerto Rican legend, on the night of April 30, 1797, the townswomen, led by a bishop, formed a rogativa, prayer procession, and marched throughout the streets of the city singing hymns and carrying torches while at the same time praying for the deliverance of the city.

Outside the walls, the invaders mistook the torch lit movement for the arrival of Spanish reinforcements.

When morning came, the enemy was gone from the island and the city was saved from a possible invasion. Four statues, sculptured by Lindsay Daen in the Plazuela de la Rogativa, Rogativa Plaza, in Old San Juan, pay tribute to the bishop and townswomen who participated in La Rogativa.

Attack of Aguadilla

The British also attacked Aguadilla and Punta Salinas. They were defeated by Colonel Conti and the members of the militia in Aguadilla, and the British troops that had landed on the island were taken prisoner.

The British retreated on April 30 to their ships and on May 2 set sail northward. Because of the defeat given to the British forces, Governor Ramon de Castro petitioned Spanish King Charles IV for recognition for the victors; he was promoted to field marshal and several others were promoted and given pay raises.

The British persisted in invading Puerto Rico, after Abercromby's defeat, with unsuccessful skirmishes on the coastal towns of Aguadilla (December 1797), Ponce, Cabo Rojo, and Mayagüez. This continued to occur until 1802 when the Treaty of Amiens ended the War of the Second Coalition between European powers and Revolutionary France.

19th century
Field Marshal Demetrio O'Daly

France had threatened to invade the Spanish colony of Santo Domingo. In 1808, the Spanish Crown sent their Navy, under the command of Puerto Rican Captain Ramón Power y Giralt, to prevent the invasion of Santo Domingo by the French by enforcing a blockade.

Col. Rafael Conti organized a military expedition with the intention of defending the Dominican Republic. They were successful and were proclaimed as heroes by the Spanish Government.

San Juan native Demetrio O'Daly was a Sergeant Major in the Spanish Army when he participated in the 1809 Peninsular War, also known as the Spanish War of Independence, after the Napoleonic Invasion of 1808 and the kidnapping of both King Charles IV and Prince Ferdinand, later King Ferdinand VII.

When King Ferdinand returned from exile and kidnapping, he repealed the Constitution of 1812, which as the rest of European monarchs, he felt was a

Napoleonic maneuver to weaken the countries. But O'Daly was a defender of the Spanish Constitution of 1812 and was considered a rebel and exiled from Spain by King Fernando VII in 1814.

In 1820 O'Daly, a liberal constitutionalist, together with fellow rebel Col. Rafael Riego organized and led the Revolt of the Colonels.

It was not a revolt against the king, but a revolt to force him to reinstate the constitution which was successful. This was called the Trienio Liberal/Liberal Three years, 1820–1823.

During this process O'Daly was promoted to field marshal and awarded the Cruz Laureada de San Fernando, Laureate Cross of Saint Ferdinand, the highest military decoration awarded by the Spanish government.

American Civil War
Lieutenant Augusto Rodríguez

During the 1800s, commerce existed between the ports of the eastern coast of the United States and Puerto Rico. Ship records show that many Puerto Ricans traveled on ships that sailed to and from the U.S. and Puerto Rico.

Many of them settled in places such as New York, Connecticut, and Massachusetts. Upon the outbreak of the American Civil War, many Puerto Ricans joined the ranks of the United States military armed forces, however since Puerto Ricans were Spanish subjects they were inscribed as Spaniards.

The 1860 census of New Haven, Connecticut, shows there were 10 Puerto Ricans living there.

Among them was Augusto Rodriguez who joined the 15th Connecticut Regiment, Lyon Regiment, in 1862.

During the Civil War, Rodriguez, who reached the rank of lieutenant, served in the defenses of Washington, D.C. He also led his men in the Battles of Fredericksburg and Wyse Fork. The regiment was mustered out on June 27, 1865, and he was discharged in New Haven on July 12, 1865.

Slave revolts

Slavery was abolished in Puerto Rico in 1873, but the wealth amassed by many landowners in Puerto Rico through a plantation economy was generated by the exploitation of slaves.

According to one source, this reliance on slavery "generated its antithesis disobedience, uprisings and flights."

In Puerto Rico, there were many minor slave revolts in which the slaves clashed with the military establishment.

In July 1821, Marcos Xiorro, a bozal slave, planned and organized a conspiracy against the slave masters and the colonial government of Puerto Rico.

According to his plot, which was to be carried out on July 27, during the festival celebrations for Santiago, St. James, several slaves were to escape from various plantations in Bayamón, which included the haciendas of Angus McBean, C. Fortnight, Miguel Andino and Fernando Fernández.

They were then to proceed to the sugarcane fields of Miguel Figueres and retrieve cutlasses and swords which were hidden in those fields.

Xiorro, together with a slave from the McBean plantation named Mario and another slave named Narciso, would lead the slaves of Bayamón and Toa Baja and capture the city of Bayamón.

They would then burn the city and kill those who were not black. After this, they would all unite with slaves from the adjoining towns of Río Piedras, Guaynabo, and Palo Seco.

With this critical mass of slaves, all armed and emboldened from a series of quick victories, they would then invade the capital city of San Juan, where they would declare Xiorro as their king.

Unfortunately for the slave conspirators, the plot was divulged by a fellow slave to the authorities.

In response, the mayor of Bayamón mobilized 500 soldiers. The ringleaders and followers of the conspiracy were captured immediately.

A total of 61 slaves were imprisoned in Bayamón and San Juan. The ringleaders were executed and the fate of Xiorro remains a mystery.

There were other minor revolts up until the abolition of slavery in the island became official.

CHAPTER 46

Revolt against Spain

South America
General Antonio Valero de Bernabé,
the "Liberator from Puerto Rico"

In 1822, there was an attempt, known as the Ducoudray Holstein Expedition, conceived, carefully planned, and organized by General Henri La Fayette Villaume Ducoudray Holstein to invade Puerto Rico and declare it a republic.

This invasion was different from all its precursors since none before had intended to make Puerto Rico an independent nation and use the Taino name "Boricua" as the official name of the republic, it was also intended more as a mercantile venture than a patriotic endeavor.

It was the first time an invasion intended to make the city of Mayagüez the capital of the island. However, plans of the invasion were soon disclosed to the Spanish authorities and the plot never materialized.

United Provinces of New Granada

In the early 19th century, the Spanish colonies, in what is known as the Latin American wars of independence, began to revolt against Spanish rule.

Antonio Valero de Bernabé was a Puerto Rican military leader known in Latin America as the "Liberator from Puerto Rico". Valero was a recent graduate of the Spanish Military Academy when Napoleon Bonaparte convinced King Charles IV of Spain to permit him to pass through Spanish soil with the sole purpose of attacking Portugal.

When Napoleon refused to leave, the Spanish government declared war. Valero joined the Spanish Army and helped defeat Napoleon's army at the siege of Saragossa. Valero became a hero; he was promoted to the rank of colonel and was awarded many decorations.

When Ferdinand VII assumed the throne of Spain in 1813, Valero became critical of the new king's policies towards the Spanish colonies in Latin America. He developed a keen hatred of the monarchy, resigned his commission in the army, and headed for Mexico.

There he joined the insurgent army headed by Agustín de Iturbide, in which Valero was named chief of staff. He fought for and helped achieve Mexico's independence from Spain. After the Mexican victory, Iturbide proclaimed himself Emperor of Mexico.

Since Valero had developed anti-monarchist feelings following his experiences in Spain, he revolted against Iturbide. His revolt failed and he attempted to escape from Mexico by way of sea.

Valero was captured by a Spanish pirate, who turned him over to the Spanish authorities in Cuba. Valero was imprisoned but managed to escape with the help of a group of men that identified with Simón Bolívar's ideals.

Upon learning of Bolívar's dream of creating a unified Latin America, including Puerto Rico and Cuba, Valero decided to join him. Valero stopped in St. Thomas, where he established contacts with the Puerto Rican independence movement.

He then traveled to Venezuela, where he was met by General Francisco de Paula Santander.

He next joined Bolívar and fought alongside "The Liberator" against Spain, gaining his confidence and admiration. Valero was named Military

Chief of the Department of Panama, Governor of Puerto Cabello, Chief of Staff of Colombia, Minister of War and Maritime of Venezuela, and in 1849 was promoted to the rank of brigadier general.

CHAPTER 47

María de las Mercedes Barbudo

The meetings of the Puerto Rican Independence movement which met in St. Thomas were discovered by the Spanish authorities and the members of the movement were either imprisoned or exiled.

In a letter dated October 1, 1824, which Venezuelan rebel leader José María Rojas sent to María de las Mercedes Barbudo, Rojas stated that the Venezuelan rebels had lost their principal contact with the Puerto Rican Independence movement in the Danish Island of Saint Thomas and therefore the secret communication which existed between the Venezuelan rebels and the leaders of the Puerto Rican independence movements was in danger of being discovered.

Mercedes Barbudo, also known as the "first Puerto Rican female freedom fighter", was a businesswoman who became a follower of the independence ideal for Puerto Rico upon learning that Bolivar dreamed of eventually engendering an American Revolution-style federation, that would be known as the United Provinces of New Granada, between all the newly independent republics, with a government ideally set-up solely to recognize and uphold individual rights.

She was involved with the Puerto Rican Independence Movement which had ties with the Venezuelan rebels led by Simón Bolívar and who were against Spanish colonial rule in Puerto Rico.

Unknown to Mercedes Barbudo, the Spanish authorities in Puerto Rico under Governor Miguel de la Torre, were suspicious of the correspondence between her and the rebel factions of Venezuela.

Secret agents of the Spanish Government had retained some of her mail and delivered it to Governor de la Torre. He ordered an investigation and had her mail confiscated.

The Government believed that the correspondence served as propaganda of the Bolivian ideals and that it would also serve to motivate Puerto Ricans to seek their independence.

Governor Miguel de la Torre ordered her arrest on the charge that she planned to overthrow the Spanish Government in Puerto Rico.

Since Puerto Rico did not have a women's prison, she was held without bail at the Castillo San Cristóbal. Among the evidence which the Spanish authorities presented against her was Rojas letter.

She was exiled to Cuba, where she was able to escape and make her way to Venezuela, where she spent her final days.

CHAPTER 48

Puerto Rico

Fort San Cristóbal Cannon

The Spanish government had received many complaints from the nations whose ships were attacked by Puerto Rican pirate Captain Roberto Cofresí. Cofresí and his men had attacked eight ships, amongst them an American ship.

The Spanish government, which routinely encouraged piracy against other nations, was pressured and felt obliged to pursue and capture the famous pirate.

In 1824, Captain John Slout of the U.S. Naval Forces and his schooner USS Grampus engaged Cofresí in a fierce battle. The pirate Cofresí was captured, along with eleven of his crew members, and turned over to the Spanish Government. He was imprisoned in El Castillo del Morro in San Juan.

Cofresí was judged by a Spanish Council of War, found guilty, and executed by firing squad on March 29, 1825.

On April 13, 1855, a mutiny broke out among the artillerymen at Fort San Cristóbal. They were protesting an extended two years of military service imposed by the island's Spanish governor, Garcia Cambia.

The mutineers pointed their cannons towards San Juan, creating a state of panic among the population. Upon their surrender, the governor had the eight men arrested and sentenced to death by firing squad.

Grito de Lares

Many Spanish colonies had gained their independence by the mid-1850s. In Puerto Rico, there were two groups: the loyalists, who were loyal to Spain, and the independentistas, who advocated independence.

In 1866, Dr. Ramón Emeterio Betances, Segundo Ruiz Belvis, and other independence advocates met in New York City where they founded the Revolutionary Committee of Puerto Rico. An outcome of this venture was a plan to send an armed expedition from the Dominican Republic to invade the island.

Several revolutionary cells were formed in the western towns and cities of Puerto Rico. Two of the most important cells were at Mayagüez, led by Mathias Brugman and code-named "Capa Prieto" and at Lares, code-named "Centro Bravo" and headed by Manuel Rojas.

"Centro Bravo" was the main center of operations and was in the Rojas plantation of El Triunfo. Manuel Rojas was named "Commander of the Liberation Army" by Betances.

Mariana Bracetti, sister-in-law of Manuel, was named "Leader of the Lares Revolutionary Council." Upon the request of Betances, Bracetti knitted the first flag of Puerto Rico also known as the revolutionary Flag of Lares, Bandera de Lares.

CHAPTER 49

Ramón Emeterio Betances

The Spanish authorities discovered the plot and were able to confiscate Betances's armed ship before it arrived in Puerto Rico.

The mayor of the town of Camuy, Manuel González, leader of that town's revolutionary cell, was arrested and charged with treason.

He learned that the Spanish Army was aware of the independence plot and escaped to warn Manuel Rojas.

Alerted, the revolutionists decided to start the revolution as soon as possible, and set the date for September 28, 1868. Mathias Brugman and his men joined with Manuel Rojas's men and with about 800 men and women, marched on and took the town of Lares. This was to be known as "Grito de Lares", The Cry of Lares.

The revolutionists entered the town's church and placed Mariana Bracetti's revolutionary flag on the High Altar as a sign that the revolution had begun.

They declared Puerto Rico to be the "Republic of Puerto Rico" and named Francisco Ramírez its President. Manuel and his poorly armed followers proceeded to march on to the town of San Sebastián, armed only with clubs and machetes.

The Spanish Army had been forewarned and awaited with superior firepower. The revolutionists were met with deadly fire. The revolt failed, many revolutionists were killed, and at least 475, including Manuel

Rojas and Mariana Bracetti, were imprisoned in the jail of Arecibo, and sentenced to death.

Others fled and went into hiding. Mathias Brugman was hiding in a local farm where he was betrayed by a farmer named Francisco Quiñones; he was captured and executed on the spot.

In 1869, fearing another revolt, the Spanish Crown disbanded the Puerto Rican Militia, which had been composed almost entirely of native-born Puerto Ricans, and the Compañia de Artilleros Morenos de Cangrejos, a separate company of black Puerto Ricans. They then organized the Volunteer Institute, composed entirely of Spaniards and their sons.

CHAPTER 50

Intentona de Yauco

During the Intentona de Yauco, the current Puerto Rican Flag was flown on the island for the first time.

Leaders of El Grito de Lares who were in exile in New York City joined the Puerto Rican Revolutionary Committee, founded on December 8, 1895, to continue the quest for independence.

In 1897, with the aid of Antonio Mattei Lluberas and Fidel Velez, the local leaders of the independence movement of the town of Yauco, they organized another uprising, which became known as the Intentona de Yauco.

On March 26, 1897, there was a second and last major attempt to overthrow the Spanish government.

The local conservative political factions, which believed that such an attempt would be a threat to their struggle for autonomy, opposed such an action.

Rumors of the planned event spread to the local Spanish authorities, who acted swiftly and put an end to what would be the last major uprising in the island to Spanish colonial rule.

CHAPTER 51

Cuba

General Juan Ríus Rivera, Commander-in-Chief of the Cuban Liberation Army

In 1869, the incoming governor of Puerto Rico, Jose Laureano Sanz, to ease tensions in the island, dictated a general amnesty and released all who were involved with the Grito de Lares revolt from prison.

Both Mariana Bracetti and Manuel Rojas were released. Bracetti lived her last years in the town of Añasco, while Rojas was deported to Venezuela.

Many of the former prisoners joined the Cuban Liberation Army and fought against Spain. Among the many Puerto Ricans who volunteered to fight for Cuba's independence were Juan Ríus Rivera, Francisco Gonzalo Marín, also known as "Pachin Marín" and José Semidei Rodríguez.

Juan Ríus Rivera as a young man met and befriended Betances. He eventually joined the pro-independence movement in the island.

He became a member of the Mayagüez revolutionary cell "Capá Prieto" under the command of Brugman.

Ríus, did not participate directly in the revolt because at the time he was studying law in Spain, however, he was an avid reader about information pertaining to the Antilles and learned about the failed revolt.

He interrupted his studies and traveled to the United States where he went to the Cuba Revolutionary "Junta" and offered his services. He joined the Cuban Liberation Army and was given the rank of general and fought alongside Gen. Máximo Gómez in Cuba's Ten Years' War.

He later fought alongside Gen. Antonio Maceo Grajales and upon Maceo's death was named Commander-in-Chief of the Cuban Liberation Army. After Cuba gained its independence, Gen. Juan Ríus Rivera became an active political figure in the new nation.

Francisco Gonzalo Marín was a poet and journalist in Puerto Rico who joined the Cuban Liberation Army upon learning of the death of his brother Wecenlao in the battlefields of Cuba.

Marin, who was given the rank of lieutenant, befriended, and fought alongside José Martí. In November 1897, Lt. Marin died from the wounds he received in a skirmish against the Spanish Army.

José Semidei Rodríguez from Yauco, Puerto Rico, fought in various battles in the Cuban War of Independence, 1895–1898. After Cuba gained its independence, he joined the Cuban National Army with the rank of brigadier general. Semidei Rodríguez continued to serve in Cuba as a diplomat upon his retirement from the military.

Spanish American War

In 1890, Captain Alfred Thayer Mahan, a member of the Navy War Board and leading U.S. strategic thinker, wrote a book titled The Influence of Sea Power upon History where he argued for the creation of a large and powerful navy modeled after the British Royal Navy.

Part of his strategy called for the acquisition of colonies in the Caribbean Sea which would serve as coaling and naval stations, and which would serve as strategic points of defense upon the construction of a canal in the Isthmus.

This was not a new idea: William H. Seward, the former Secretary of State under the administrations of various presidents, among them Abraham Lincoln and Ulysses Grant, had stressed that a canal be built either in Honduras, Nicaragua, or Panama and that the United States annex the Dominican Republic and purchase Puerto Rico and Cuba.

The idea of annexing the Dominican Republic failed to receive the approval of the U.S. Senate and Spain did not accept the 160 million dollars the U.S. offered for Puerto Rico and Cuba.

Since 1894 the Naval War College had been formulating plans for war with possible adversaries. One of these plans included military operations in Puerto Rican waters.

Not only was Puerto Rico considered valuable as a naval station, Puerto Rico and Cuba were also major producers of sugar, a valuable commercial commodity the United States lacked.

The United States declared war on Spain in 1898 following the loss of the battleship USS Maine in Havana harbor, Cuba. One of the United States' principal objectives in the Spanish American War was to take control of Spanish possessions Puerto Rico and Cuba in the Atlantic, and the Philippines and Guam in the Pacific.

The Spanish sent the 1st, 2nd, and 3rd Puerto Rican Provisional Battalions to defend Cuba against the American invaders.

The 1st Puerto Rican Provisional Battalion, composed of the Talavera Cavalry and Krupp artillery, was sent to Santiago de Cuba where they fought American forces in the Battle of San Juan Hill.

The Puerto Rican Battalion suffered a total of 70% casualties including dead, wounded, MIAs and prisoners.

The invasion of Puerto Rico by the American military forces was known as the Puerto Rican Campaign.

On May 10, 1898, Spanish forces under the command of Captain Ángel Rivero Méndez in the fortress of San Cristóbal in San Juan, exchanged fire with the USS Yale, and on May 12 a fleet of 12 American ships bombarded San Juan.

On June 25, the USS Yosemite arrived in San Juan and blockaded the port. Captains Ramón Acha Camaño and José Antonio Iriarte, both natives of Puerto Rico, were among those who defended the city from Fort San Felipe del Morro.

They had three batteries under their command, which were armed with at least three 15 cm Ordóñez cannons.

The battle lasted three hours and resulted in the death of Justo Esquivies, the first Puerto Rican soldier to die in the Puerto Rican Campaign.

On July 25, General Nelson A. Miles landed at the southern town of Guánica and began advancing towards Ponce and then San Juan.

Part of the Hacienda Desideria, owned by Antonio Mariani, where the Battle of Yauco took place in 1898.

One of the most notable battles during the Puerto Rico Campaign occurred between combined Spanish forces and Puerto Rican volunteers, led by Captain Salvador Meca and Lieutenant Colonel Francisco Puig, and American forces led by Brigadier General George A. Garretson on July 26, 1898.

The Spanish forces engaged the 6th Massachusetts in the Battle of Yauco. Puig and his forces suffered 2 officers and 3 soldiers wounded and 2 soldiers dead. The Spanish forces were ordered to retreat.

The Puerto Rican Campaign was short compared to the other campaigns because the Puerto Ricans who resided in the southern and western towns and villages resented Spanish rule and tended to view the Americans as their liberators, thereby making the invasion much easier.

The 1st, 2nd and 3rd Puerto Rican Provisional Battalions were in Cuba defending that island, which may have also contributed.

However, the Americans met resistance from the Spanish forces and Puerto Rican Volunteers and were engaged in the following battles: Battle of Fajardo, Battle of Guayama, Battle of the Guamani River Bridge, Battle of Coamo, Battle of Silva Heights and Battle of Asomante.

On August 13, 1898, the Spanish American War ended, and the Spanish surrendered without other major incidents. Some Puerto Rican leaders such as José de Diego and Eugenio María de Hostos expected the United States to grant the island its independence.

Believing that Puerto Rico would gain its independence, a group of men staged an uprising in Ciales which became known as

"El Levantamiento de Ciales" or the "Ciales Uprising of 1898" and proclaimed Puerto Rico to be a republic.

The Spanish authorities who were unaware that the cease fire had been signed brutally suppressed the uprising.

The total casualties of the Puerto Rican Campaign were 450 dead or wounded Spanish and Puerto Ricans, and 4 dead and 39 wounded Americans.

Upon the signing of the Treaty of Paris on December 10, Puerto Rico became a territory of the United States. The Spanish troops had already left by October 18, and the United States named General Nelson A. Miles military governor of the island.

On July 1, 1899, "The Porto Rico Regiment of Infantry, United States Army" was created, and approved by the U.S. Congress on May 27, 1908. The regiment was a segregated, all-volunteer unit made up of 1,969 Puerto Ricans.

Puerto Rican commander in the Philippines

In 1897, before the onset of fighting in Puerto Rico, Juan Alonso Zayas, born in San Juan, was a second lieutenant in the Spanish Army when he received orders to head for the Philippines to take command of the 2nd Expeditionary Battalion stationed in Baler. He arrived in Manila, the capital, in May 1897.

There, he took a vessel and headed for Baler, on the island of Luzon. The distance between Manila and Baler is 62 miles, 100 km; if traveled through the jungles and badly built roads, the actual distance was 144 miles, 230 km.

At that time a system of communication between Manila and Baler was almost non-existent. The only way Baler received news from Manila was by way of vessels.

The Spanish colonial government was under constant attack from local Filipino groups who wanted independence. Zayas's mission was to fortify Baler against any possible attack. Among his plans for the defense of Baler was to convert the local church of San Luis de Tolosa into a fort.

The independence advocates, under the leadership of Colonel Calixto Vilacorte, were called "insurgents", Tagalos, by the Spanish.

On June 28, 1898, they demanded the surrender of the Spanish army. The Spanish governor of the region, Enrique de las Morena y Fossi, refused.

The Filipinos immediately attacked Baler in a battle that was to last for seven months. Despite being outnumbered and suffering hunger and disease, the battalion did not capitulate. In the meantime, Zayas and the rest of the battalion were totally unaware of the Spanish American War.

In August 1898, hostilities between the United States and Spain came to an end. The Philippines became a U.S. possession in accordance with the Treaty of Paris.

In May 1899, the battalion at Baler learned of the Spanish American War and its aftermath.

On June 2, 1899, the battalion's commander, Lieutenant Martín Cerezo, surrendered to the Tagalos.

The surrender was dependent upon several conditions, including the Spaniards not being treated as prisoners of war and being allowed to travel to a ship that would take them back to Spain.

The 32 survivors of Zayas Battalion were sent to Manila, where they boarded a ship for Spain. In Spain, they were given a hero's welcome and became known as los Ultimos de Baler "the Last of Baler".

Porto Rico Provisional Regiment of Infantry

On March 2, 1898, Congress authorized the creation of the first body of native troops in Puerto Rico. On June 30, 1901, the "Porto Rico Provisional Regiment of Infantry" came into being.

An Act of Congress, approved on May 27, 1908, reorganized the regiment as part of the "regular" Army. Since the native Puerto Rican officers were Puerto Rican citizens and not citizens of the United States, they were required to undergo a new physical examination to determine their fitness for commissions in the Regular Army and to take an oath of U.S. citizenship with their new officers oath.

CHAPTER 52

Puerto Rico National Guard

Major General Luis R. Esteves (Army)

In 1906, a group of Puerto Ricans met with the appointed Governor Winthrop, and suggested the organization of a Puerto Rico National Guard.

The petition failed because the U.S. Constitution prohibits the formation of any armed force within the United States and its territories without the authorization of Congress.

On June 19, 1915, Major General Luis R. Esteves of the U.S. Army became the first Puerto Rican and the first Hispanic to graduate from the United States Military Academy at West Point, New York.

While he attended West Point, he tutored classmate Dwight D. Eisenhower in Spanish; a second language was required to graduate. He was a second lieutenant in the 8th Infantry Brigade under the command of John J. Pershing when he was sent to El Paso, Texas, in the Pancho Villa Expedition.

From El Paso, he was sent to the town of Polvo, where he was appointed mayor and judge by its citizens. Esteves helped organize the 23rd Battalion, which would be composed of Puerto Ricans and be stationed in Panama during World War I. He also played a key role in the formation of the Puerto Rico National Guard.

World War I

In 1904, Camp Las Casas was established in Santurce under the command of Lt. Colonel Orval P. Townshend. The Porto Rico Regiment was assigned to the camp. The regiment consisted of two battalions of the former Porto Rico Provisional Regiment of Infantry.

Lieutenant Teófilo Marxuach was the officer of the day at El Morro Castle on March 21, 1915. The Odenwald, built in 1903, not to be confused with the German World War II war ship which carried the same name, was an armed German supply ship which tried to force its way out of the San Juan Bay and deliver supplies to the German submarines waiting in the Atlantic Ocean.

Lt. Marxuach gave the order to open fire on the ship from the walls of the fort. Sergeant Encarnacion Correa manned a machine gun and fired warning shots with little effect.

Marxuach fired a shot from a cannon located at the Santa Rosa battery of "El Morro" fort, in what is the first shot of World War I fired by the regular armed forces of the United States against any ship flying the colors of the Central Powers, forcing the Odenwald to stop and to return to port where its supplies were confiscated.

The Odenwald was confiscated by the United States and renamed SS Newport. It was assigned to the U.S. Shipping Board, where it served until 1924 when it was retired.

As more countries became involved in World War I, the U.S. Congress approved the Jones–Shafroth Act, which imposed United States citizenship upon Puerto Ricans.

Those who were eligible, except for women, were expected to serve in the military. About 20,000 Puerto Ricans were drafted during World War I.

On May 3, 1917, the regiment recruited 1,969 men. The 295th and 296 Infantry Regiments were created in Puerto Rico.

In November 1917, the first military draft, conscription, lottery in Puerto Rico was held in the island's capital, San Juan.

Eustaquio Correa was the first Puerto Rican to be drafted into the Armed Forces of the United States.

On May 17, 1917, the Porto Rico Regiment of Infantry was deployed to guard the Panama Canal. One of the Puerto Ricans who distinguished himself during World War I was Lieutenant Frederick Lois Riefkohl of the US Navy, who on August 2, 1917, became the first known Puerto Rican to be awarded the Navy Cross.

The Navy Cross was awarded to Lt. Riefkohl for his actions in an engagement with an enemy submarine. Lt. Riefkohl, who was also the first Puerto Rican to graduate from the United States Naval Academy, served as a rear admiral in World War II.

Frederick L. Riefkohl's brother, Rudolph William Riefkohl also served. Riefkohl was commissioned a second lieutenant and assigned to the 63rd Heavy Artillery Regiment in France, where he participated in the Meuse-Argonne Offensive.

According to the United States War Department, after the war he served as Captain of Coastal Artillery at the Letterman Army Medical Center in Presidio of San Francisco, in California, 1918. He played an instrumental role in helping the people of Poland overcome the 1919 typhus epidemic.

By 1918, the Army realized there was a shortage of physicians specializing in anesthesia, a low salary specialty, who were required in military operating rooms. To address the need, the Army began hiring women physicians as civilian contract employees.

The first Puerto Rican woman doctor to serve in the Army under contract was Dr. Dolores Piñero from San Juan. She was assigned to the San Juan base hospital where she worked as an anesthesiologist during the mornings and in the laboratory during the afternoons.

In New York, some Puerto Ricans joined the 369th Infantry Regiment, which was mostly composed of African Americans. They were not allowed to fight alongside their white counterparts but did serve as part of a French division.

They fought on the Western Front in France, and their reputation earned them the nickname of "the Harlem Hell Fighters" by the Germans.

Among them was Rafael Hernández Marín, considered by many as Puerto Rico's greatest composer.

The 369th was awarded French Croix de guerre for battlefield gallantry by the French government.

On January 6, 1914, First Lieutenant Bernard L. Smith established the Marine Section of the Navy Flying School in the island municipal Culebra.

As the number of Marine Aviators grew so did the desire to separate from Naval Aviation.

The Marine Corps Aviation Company in Puerto Rico consisted of 10 officers and 40 enlisted men.

The first USMC plane was a Curtiss C-3 in Culebra, Puerto Rico

The Porto Rico Regiment returned to Puerto Rico in March 1919 and was renamed the 65th Infantry Regiment under the Reorganization Act of June 4, 1920.

It is estimated that 18,000 Puerto Ricans from the Porto Rico Regiment served in the war and that 335 were wounded by chemical gas experimentation the United States conducted as part of its active chemical weapons program in Panama.

Neither the military nor the War Department of the United States kept statistics regarding the total number of Puerto Ricans who served in the regular units of the Armed Forces, United States mainland forces.

It is known that four Puerto Ricans died in combat, but it is impossible to determine the exact number of Puerto Ricans who served and died in World War I.

The need for a Puerto Rican National Guard unit became apparent to Major General Luis R. Esteves, who had served as an instructor of Puerto Rican Officers for the Porto Rico Regiment of Infantry at Camp

Las Casas in Puerto Rico. His request was approved by the government and Puerto Rican Legislature.

In 1919, the first regiment of the Puerto Rican National Guard was formed, and General Luis R. Esteves became the first official Commandant of the Puerto Rican National Guard.

Interwar years
Second Nicaraguan Campaign (1926–1933)

After World War I, Puerto Ricans fought on foreign shores as members of the United States Marine Corps. Civil war broke out in Nicaragua during the first months of 1926, and upon the request of the Nicaraguan government, 3,000 U.S.

Marines were sent ashore to establish a neutral zone for the protection of American citizens. The American intervention was also known as the Banana Wars.

In 1926, Captain Pedro del Valle served with the Gendarmerie of Haiti for three years. During that time, he also became active in the war against Augusto Sandino in Nicaragua.

In 1927, Lieutenant Jaime Sabater, from San Juan, Puerto Rico, graduated from United States Naval Academy.

Private Rafael Toro, from Humacao, Puerto Rico, was part of the U.S. Marine Corps occupation force in Nicaragua, serving with the Guardia Nacional de Nicaragua.

On July 25, 1927, Private Toro was assigned to advance guard duty in Nueva Segovia. As he rode into town, he was attacked; returning fire, he was able to hold back the enemy until reinforcements arrived.

He was mortally wounded in this action and was posthumously awarded the Navy Cross.

Rif War 1920

After the Spanish American War, members of the Spanish forces and civilians who were loyal to the Spanish Crown were allowed to return to Spain.

Those who returned took with them their Puerto Rican spouses and children. Among those who were born in Puerto Rico and who would go on to serve in the Rif War as members of the Spanish military were General Manuel Goded Llopis and Captain Felix Arenas Gaspar.

The Rif War was a rebellion against Spanish colonial rule in Spanish Morocco, a Spanish protectorate, in 1919.

During the Rif War Gaspar, who was born in San Juan, distinguished himself in combat. He was posthumously awarded the Cruz Laureada de San Fernando "Laureate Cross of Saint Ferdinand" Spain's version of the United States' Medal of Honor for his actions in the defense of his company.

CHAPTER 53

Spanish Civil War 1936–1939

Puerto Ricans fought on both sides during the Spanish Civil War. The Spanish Civil War was a major conflict in Spain that started after an attempted coup d'état by parts of the army, led by the Fascist General Francisco Franco, against the government of the Second Spanish Republic.

Puerto Ricans fought on both factions involved; the "Nationalists" as members of the Spanish Army and the "Loyalists", Republicans, as members of the Abraham Lincoln International Brigade.

Among the Puerto Ricans who fought alongside General Franco and the Nationalists was General Manuel Goded Llopis, 1882–1936.

Llopis, who was born in San Juan, was named Chief of Staff of the Spanish Army of Africa after his victories in the Rif War, took the Balearic Islands and by order of Franco, suppressed the rebellion of Asturias.

Llopis was sent to lead the fight against the Anarchists in Catalonia, but his troops were outnumbered. He was captured and was sentenced to die by firing squad.

Among the many Puerto Ricans who fought for the Second Spanish Republic as members of the Abraham Lincoln Brigade was Lieutenant Carmelo Delgado Delgado, 1913–1937, a leader of the Puerto Rican Nationalist Party from Guayama.

At the start of the Spanish Civil War Delgado was in Spain studying for a law degree. Delgado was an anti-fascist who believed the Spanish Nationalists were traitors. He fought in the Battle of Madrid but was captured and sentenced to die by firing squad on April 29, 1937.

World War II
Pearl Harbor of the Atlantic

In 1940, when Germany attacked Great Britain, President Franklin Delano Roosevelt ordered the construction of a protected anchorage in the Atlantic, at Ceiba, Puerto Rico, like Pearl Harbor in Hawaii.

The site was meant to provide anchorage, docking, repair facilities, fuel, and supplies for 60% of the Atlantic Fleet. The naval base, which was named U.S. Naval Station Roosevelt Roads, became the largest naval installation in the world in landmass. In May 2003, after six decades of existence, the base was officially shut down by the U.S. Navy.

In 1939, a survey was conducted of possible air base sites. It was determined that Punta Borinquen was the best site for a major air base. Later that year, Major Karl S. Axtater assumed command of what was to become Borinquen Army Airfield, later renamed Ramey Air Force Base.

The first squadron based at Borinquen Field was the 27th Bombardment Squadron, consisting of nine Douglas B-18A Bolo medium bombers.

In 1940, the air echelon of the 25th Bombardment Group, 14 B-18A aircraft and two Northrop A-17 aircraft, arrived at the base from Langley Field.

Throughout the war, many squadrons rotated through the airbase, which was supported by numerous antiaircraft, coastal artillery and support units.

Borinquen Field was also used as a part of the ferrying route for aircraft being moved from Florida to the Middle East.

PBM Mariners taking off from Naval Air Station San Juan in 1943 Puerto Ricans in the military

In October 1940, the 295th and 296th Infantry Regiments of the Puerto Rican National Guard, founded by Major General Luis R. Esteves, were called into Federal Active Service, and assigned to the Puerto Rican Department in accordance with the existing War Plan Orange.

There were no Puerto Rican military-related fatalities in the Japanese attack of Pearl Harbor, although one Puerto Rican civilian was killed.

Daniel LaVerne was an amateur boxer who was working at Pearl Harbor's Red Hill underground fuel tank construction project when the Japanese attacked.

He died because of the injuries which he received during the attack. His name is listed among the 2,338 Americans killed or mortally wounded on December 7, 1941, in the Remembrance Exhibit on the back lawn of the USS Arizona Memorial Visitor Center at Pearl Harbor.

It is estimated by the Department of Defense that 65,034 Puerto Ricans served in the U.S. military during World War II.

Soldiers from the island, serving in the 65th Infantry Regiment, participated in combat in the European Theater, in Germany and Central Europe.

Those who resided in the mainland of the United States were assigned to regular units of the military and served either in the European or Pacific theaters of the war.

Some families had multiple members join the Armed Forces. Seven brothers of the Medina family known as "The Fighting Medinas", fought in the war.

They came from Río Grande, Puerto Rico, and Brooklyn, New York. In some cases, Puerto Ricans were subject to the racial discrimination which at that time was widespread in the United States.

CHAPTER 54

"The Fighting Medinas"

World War II was also the first conflict in which women, other than nurses, were allowed to serve in the U.S. Armed Forces.

However, when the United States entered World War II, Puerto Rican nurses volunteered for service but were not accepted into the Army or Navy Nurse Corps.

As a result, many of the volunteers migrated to the mainland U.S. to work in the factories which produced military equipment.

In 1944, the Army Nurse Corps decided to actively recruit Puerto Rican nurses so that Army hospitals would not have to deal with the language barriers when tending to wound Hispanic soldiers.

Among them was Second Lieutenant Carmen Lozano Dumler, who became one of the first Puerto Rican female military officers.

In 1944, the Army sought to recruit up to 200 Puerto Rican women for the Women's Army Corps (WAC). Over 1,000 applications were received. The Puerto Rican WAC unit, designated Company 6, 2nd Battalion, 21st Regiment of the Women's Army Auxiliary Corps, was a segregated Hispanic unit.

It was assigned to the New York Port of Embarkation after basic training at Fort Oglethorpe, Georgia. The WACs were assigned to work in military offices which planned the shipment of troops around the world.

Among them was PFC Carmen García Rosado, who in 2006, authored and published a book titled "LAS WACS, Participacion de la Mujer Boricua en la Segunda Guerra Mundial" The WACs, the participation of the Puerto Rican women in the Second World War, the first book to document the experiences of the first 200 Puerto Rican women who participated in said conflict.

According to García Rosado, one of the hardships which Puerto Rican women in the military were subjected to was social and racial discrimination against the Latino community, which at the time was rampant in the United States.

Puerto Rican Army nurses, 296th Station Hospital, Camp Tortuguero, Vega Baja, PR.

The 149th Women's Army Auxiliary Corps, WAAC, Post Headquarters Company was the first WAAC Company to go overseas, setting sail from New York Harbor for Europe in January 1943.

The unit arrived in Northern Africa on January 27, 1943, and rendered overseas duties in Algiers within General Dwight D. Eisenhower's theater headquarters. Tech4 Carmen Contreras-Bozak, a member of this unit, was the first Hispanic to serve in the Women's Army Corps as an interpreter and in numerous administrative positions.

The 65th Infantry, after an extensive training program in 1942, was sent to Panama to protect the Pacific and the Atlantic sides of the isthmus in 1943. On November 25, 1943, Colonel Antulio Segarra, proceeded Col. John R. Menclenhall as Commander of the 65th Infantry, thus becoming the first Puerto Rican Regular Army officer to command a Regular Army regiment.

On January 12, 1944, the 296th Infantry Regiment departed from Puerto Rico to the Panama Canal Zone.

In April 1945, the unit returned to Puerto Rico and soon after was sent to Honolulu, Hawaii. The 296th arrived on June 25, 1945, and was attached to the Central Pacific Base Command at Kahuku Air Base.

Lieutenant Colonel Gilberto José Marxuach, "The Father of the San Juan Civil Defense", was the commander of both the 1114th Artillery Co. and the 1558th Engineers Co.

Also in January 1944, the 65th Infantry Regiment was moved from Panama to Fort Eustis in Newport News, Virginia, in preparation for overseas deployment to North Africa. An advance party was sent to Casablanca on 16 March, with the remainder of the regiment arriving by 5 April.

For some Puerto Ricans, this would be the first time that they were away from their homeland. Being away from their homeland for the first time would serve as an inspiration for compositions of two Bolero's; "En mi viejo San Juan" by Noel Estrada and "Despedida", My Good-bye, a farewell song written by Pedro Flores and interpreted by Daniel Santos.

By April 29, 1944, the regiment had landed in Italy and moved on to Corsica. On 1 October 1944, the 65th Infantry landed in France and was committed to action on the Maritime Alps at Peira Cava.

On December 13, 1944, the 65th Infantry, under the command of Lieutenant Colonel Juan César Cordero Dávila, relieved the 2nd Battalion, 442nd Infantry Regiment, a regiment which was made up of Japanese Americans under the command of Col. Virgil R. Miller, a native of Puerto Rico.

The 3rd Battalion fought against and defeated Germany's 34th Infantry Division's 107th Infantry Regiment. There were 17 battle casualties.

These included Pvt. Sergio Sanchez-Sanchez and Sergeant Angel Martinez, from the town of Sabana Grande, who were the first two Puerto Ricans from the 65th Infantry to be killed in combat.

On March 18, 1945, the regiment was sent to the District of Mannheim and assigned to military occupation duties.

In all, the 65th Infantry participated in the campaigns of Naples-Fogis, Rome-Arno, central Europe and of the Rhineland.

It was during this conflict that CWO2 Joseph B. Aviles Sr., a member of the United States Coast Guard and the first Hispanic American to be promoted to Chief Petty Officer, "received a war-time promotion to Chief Warrant Officer, November 27, 1944, thus becoming the first Hispanic American to reach that level as well.

"Aviles, who served in the United States Navy as Chief Gunner's Mate in World War I, spent most of the war at St. Augustine, Florida, training recruits.

CHAPTER 55

Commanders

Lt. Gen. Pedro del Valle, (USMC)

This was also the first time that Puerto Ricans played important roles as commanders in the Armed Forces of the United States. Besides Lieutenant Colonel Juan César Cordero Dávila who served with the 65th Infantry and Colonel Virgil R. Miller, a West Point graduate, born in San Germán, Puerto Rico, who was the regimental commander of the 442d Regimental Combat Team, a unit which was composed of "Nisei", second generation Americans of Japanese descent, that rescued Lost Texas Battalion of the 36th Infantry Division, in the forests of the Vosges Mountains in northeastern France.

Colonel Virgilio N. Cordero Jr., 1893–1980, was a battalion commander of the 31st Infantry Regiment on December 8, 1941, when Japanese attacked Philippines. Cordero was named regimental commander of the 52nd Infantry Regiment of the new Filipino Army, thus becoming the first Puerto Rican to command a Filipino Army regiment.

The Bataan Defense Force surrendered on April 9, 1942, and Cordero and his men underwent brutal torture and humiliation during the Bataan Death March and nearly four years of captivity.

He was one of nearly 1,600 members of the 31st Infantry who were taken as prisoners. Half of these men perished while prisoners of the Japanese forces.

After Cordero gained his freedom, when the Allied troops defeated the Japanese, he continued serving in the military until 1953.

Seven Puerto Ricans, all graduates of the United States Naval Academy, served in command positions in the Navy and the Marine Corps.

Lieutenant General Pedro Augusto del Valle was the first Hispanic Marine Corps general. He played a key role in the Guadalcanal Campaign and the Battle of Guam and became the Commanding General of the First Marine Division.

Del Valle played an instrumental role in the defeat of the Japanese forces in Okinawa and oversaw the reorganization of Okinawa. Admiral Horacio Rivero Jr., USN, who later became the first Puerto Rican to become a four-star admiral; Captain Marion Frederic Ramírez de Arellano, USN, the first Hispanic submarine commanding officer.

As submarine commander of the USS Balao, SS-285, he is credited with sinking two Japanese ships; Rear Admiral Rafael Celestino Benítez, USN, a highly decorated submarine commander who was the recipient of two Silver Star Medals; Rear Admiral José M. Cabanillas, USN, who was the executive officer of the USS Texas which participated in the invasions of North Africa and Normandy, D-Day.

Rear Admiral Edmund Ernest García, USN, commander of the destroyer USS Sloat who saw action in the invasions of Africa, Sicily, and France.

Rear Admiral Frederick Lois Riefkohl, USN, the first Puerto Rican to graduate from the Naval Academy and recipient of the Navy Cross and Colonel Jaime Sabater Sr., USMC, who commanded the 1st Battalion, 9th Marines during the Bougainville amphibious operations.

Sabater also participated in the Battle of Guam, July 21 – August 10, 1944, as executive officer of the 9th Marines. He was wounded in action on July 21, 1944, and awarded the Purple Heart.

Notable combatants

Among the many Puerto Ricans who distinguished themselves in combat were Sergeant First Class Agustín Ramos Calero and the first three Puerto Ricans to be awarded the Distinguished Service Cross: PFC. Luis F. Castro, Private Anibal Irrizarry, and PFC Joseph R. Martinez.

Sergeant First Class Agustín Ramos Calero was awarded a total of 22 decorations and medals his actions in Europe, making him the most decorated Puerto Rican soldier of World War II.

Aviators
Lieutenant Colonel José Antonio Muñiz, (USAAF)

Puerto Ricans also served in the United States Army Air Forces. In 1944, Puerto Rican aviators were sent to the Tuskegee Army Airfield in Tuskegee, Alabama, to train the famed 99th Fighter Squadron of the Tuskegee Airmen.

A few Puerto Ricans who served in the Royal Canadian Air Force, the British Royal Air Force.

Human experimentation

Puerto Rican soldiers were subject to human experimentation by the United States Armed Forces. On Panama's San Jose Island, Puerto Rican soldiers were exposed to mustard gas to see if they reacted differently than their "white" counterparts.

According to Susan L. Smith of the University of Alberta, the researchers were searching for evidence of race-based differences in the responses of the human body to mustard gas exposure.

Demobilization
LTJG Maria Rodriguez Denton

The American participation in the Second World War came to an end in Europe on May 8, 1945, when the western Allies celebrated "V-E Day", Victory in Europe Day, upon Germany's surrender, and in the Asian theater on August 14, 1945 "V-J Day", Victory over Japan Day, when the Japanese surrendered by signing the Japanese Instrument of Surrender.

Lieutenant Junior Grade Maria Rodriguez Denton, U.S. Navy, born in Guanica, Puerto Rico, was the first woman from Puerto Rico who became an officer in the United States Navy as member of the WAVES. It was LTJG Denton who forwarded the news, through channels, to President Harry S. Truman that the war had ended.

On October 27, 1945, the 65th Infantry sailed home from France. Arriving at Puerto Rico on November 9, 1945, they were received by the local population as national heroes and given a victorious reception at the Military Terminal of Camp Buchanan.

According to the book "Historia Militar De Puerto Rico", Military history of Puerto Rico, by historian Col. Héctor Andrés Negroni, the men of the 65th Infantry were awarded the following military decorations: 2 Silver Stars, 22 Bronze Stars, and 90 Purple Hearts.

The 295th Regiment returned on February 20, 1946, from the Panama Canal Zone, and the 296th Regiment on March 6. Both regiments were awarded the American Theater streamer and the Pacific Theater streamer. They were inactivated that same year.

According to the 4th Report of the Director of Selective Service of 1948, a total of 51,438 Puerto Ricans served in the Armed Forces during World War II, however, the Department of Defense in its report titled "Number of Puerto Ricans serving in the U.S. Armed Forces during National Emergencies" stated that the total of Puerto Ricans who served was 65,034 and from that total 2,560 were listed as wounded.

Unfortunately, the exact total amount of Puerto Ricans who served in World War II in other units, besides those of Puerto Rico, cannot be determined because the military categorized Hispanics under the same heading as whites. The only racial groups to have separate statistics kept were African Americans and Asian Americans.

CHAPTER 56

Revolt against the United States

During the mid-1940s, various pro-independence groups, such as the Puerto Rican Independence Party, which believed in gaining the island's independence through the electoral process, and the Puerto Rican Nationalist Party, which believed in the concept of armed revolution, existed in Puerto Rico.

On October 30, 1950, the nationalists, under the leadership of Dr. Pedro Albizu Campos staged uprisings in the towns of Ponce, Mayagüez, Naranjito, Arecibo, Utuado, Utuado Uprising, San Juan, San Juan Nationalist revolt and Jayuya.

The National Guard, commanded by the Puerto Rico Adjutant General Major General Luis R. Esteves and under the orders of Gov. Luis Muñoz Marín, occupy Jayuya.

The most notable of these occurred in Jayuya in what became known as El Grito de Jayuya, Jayuya Uprising. Nationalist leader Blanca Canales led the armed nationalists into the town and attacked the police station.

A small battle with the police occurred; one officer was killed, and three others were wounded before the rest dropped their weapons and surrendered.

The nationalists cut the telephone lines and burned the post office. Canales led the group into the town square where the illegal light blue version of the Puerto Rican Flag was raised,it was against the law to carry a Puerto Rican Flag from 1898 to 1952.

In the town square, Canales gave a speech and declared Puerto Rico a free Republic. The town was held by the nationalists for three days.

The United States declared martial law in Puerto Rico and sent the Puerto Rico National Guard to attack Jayuya. The town was attacked by U.S. bomber planes and ground artillery.

Even though part of the town was destroyed, news of this military action was prevented from spreading outside of Puerto Rico. It was called an incident between Puerto Ricans. The top leaders of the nationalist party, including Albizu Campos and Blanca Canales, were arrested and sent to jail to serve long prison terms.

Griselio Torresola, Albizu Campos's bodyguard, was in the United States at the time of the Jayuya Uprising. Torresola and fellow nationalist Oscar Collazo, were to assassinate President Harry S. Truman.

On November 1, 1950, they attacked the Blair House where Torresola and a policeman, Leslie Coffelt, lost their lives. Oscar Collazo was arrested and sentenced to death. His sentence was later commuted to life imprisonment by President Truman, and he eventually received a presidential pardon.

CHAPTER 57

Cold War 1947–1991

After World War II a geopolitical, ideological, and economic struggle emerged between the United States and the Soviet Union and their respective allies. Popularly named the Cold War, open hostilities never occurred between the main parties involved. Instead, it involved a nuclear and conventional weapons arms race, networks of military alliances, economic warfare and trade embargoes, propaganda, espionage, and smaller conflicts.

The Cuban Missile Crisis of 1962 was the most important direct confrontation. The Korean and Vietnam War were among the major civil wars polarized along Cold War lines.

Puerto Rico Air National Guard

Colonel Mihiel Gilormini was named commander of the 198th Fighter Squadron in Puerto Rico. Gilormini and Colonel Alberto A. Nido, together with Lieutenant Colonel Jose Antonio Muñiz, played an instrumental role in the creation of the Puerto Rico Air National Guard on November 23, 1947. The Puerto Rico Air National Guard is a part of the Air Reserve Component, ARC, of the United States Air Force.

Both Gilormini and Nido were eventually promoted to brigadier general and served as commanders of PRANG. In 1963, the Air National Guard Base, at the San Juan International airport in Puerto Rico, was renamed "Muñiz Air National Guard Base" in honor of Lt. Col. Jose Antonio Muñiz who died on July 4, 1960, when his F-86 crashed during takeoff during the 4th of July festivities in Puerto Rico.

USS Cochino incident

The USS Cochino, SS-345, was a Gato-class submarine under the command of Commander Rafael Celestino Benítez.

On August 12, 1949, the Cochino, along with the USS Tusk, SS-426, departed from Portsmouth, United Kingdom. Both diesel submarines were supposed to be on a cold-water training mission, however, according to Blind Man's Bluff.

The Untold Story of American Submarine Espionage, the submarines were part of an American intelligence operation. They had snorkels that allowed them to spend long periods underwater, largely invisible to an enemy, and they carried electronic gear designed to detect far-off radio signals.

The mission of the Cochino and the Tusk was to eavesdrop on communications that revealed the testing of submarine-launched Soviet missiles that might soon carry nuclear warheads; it was the first American undersea spy mission of the Cold War.

The mission was cut short when one of the Cochino's 4,000-pound batteries caught fire. Benitez directed the firefighting, trying both to save the ship and his crew from the toxic gases. The crew members of the Tusk rescued all except one Cochino crew member and convinced Benitez, who was the last man on the Cochino, to board the Tusk. The Cochino sank off the coast of Norway two minutes after Benitez's departure. Benitez retired from the Navy in 1957 as a rear admiral.

Korean War

Sixty-one thousand Puerto Ricans served in the Korean War, including 18,000 Puerto Ricans who enlisted in the continental United States.

On August 26, 1950, the 65th Infantry Regiment departed from Puerto Rico and arrived in Pusan, Korea on September 23, 1950. It was during the long sea voyage that the 65th Infantry was nicknamed the "Borinqueneers".

The name is a combination of the words "Borinquen", the Taíno name for Puerto Rico and "Buccaneers".

Among the hardships suffered by the Puerto Ricans after they arrived in Korea was the lack of warm clothing during the cold, harsh winters.

The enemy made many attempts to encircle the regiment, but each time they failed because of the many casualties inflicted by the 65th.

In December 1950, U.S. Marines found themselves at the Chosin Reservoir area. The 65th was part of a task force which enabled the Marines to withdraw from Hangu-Ri.

Company "C" of the 65th Infantry on patrol

In December 1952, 162 Puerto Ricans of the 65th Infantry were arrested, 95 were court-martialed, and 91 were found guilty and sentenced to prison terms ranging from 1 to 18 years of hard labor.

It was the largest mass court martial of the Korean War. The Secretary of the Army Robert T. Stevens moved quickly to remit the sentences and granted clemency and pardons to all those involved.

Though the men who were court-martialed were pardoned in 1954, a campaign was later started to obtain a formal exoneration.

Among the battles and operations in which the 65th participated was the operation "Killer" of January 1951, becoming the first regiment to cross the Han River.

In April 1951, the regiment participated in the Uijonber Corridor drives and in June 1951, the 65th was the third regiment to cross the Han Ton River.

Master Sergeant Juan E. Negrón received the Medal of Honor posthumously on March 18, 2014, for his courageous actions while serving as a member of Company L, 65th Infantry Regiment, 3d Infantry Division during combat operations against an armed enemy in Kalma-Eri, Korea on April 28, 1951.

Members of the 2nd platoon, Company C, 65th Infantry Regiment 1952

The 65th helped push the advance from Ch'orwon towards P'yonggang in June and then assisted in breaking the Iron Triangle of Hill 717 in July 1951.

In late November 1951, the 65th successfully fought off an attack by two battalion-sized enemy units.

Colonel Juan César Cordero Dávila was named commander of 65th Infantry on February 1, 1952, thus becoming one of the highest-ranking ethnic officers in the Army.

Commencing on July 3, 1952, the regiment defended the main line of resistance, MLR, for 47 days and saw action at Cognac, King, and Queen with successful attacks on Chinese positions.

In September 1952, the 65th Infantry was holding on to a hill known as Outpost Kelly. Chinese Communist forces that had joined the North Koreans overran the hill in what became known as the Battle of Outpost Kelly.

The 65th Infantry Regiment launched several efforts to retake the position but was overwhelmed by Chinese artillery and driven off on 24 September.

In October the regiment also saw action in the Cherwon Sector and on Iron Horse, around Hill 391, which became known as Jackson Heights.

In June 1953, the 2nd Battalion, 65th Infantry Regiment conducted a series of successful raids on Hill 412 in support of a position called Outpost Harry, and later the regiment conducted several successful raids in addition to defending defensive positions near the base of the Iron Triangle until the armistice was signed in July.

The 65th Infantry was credited with battle participation in nine campaigns. Among the distinctions awarded to the members of the 65th were a Medal of Honor, 10 Distinguished Service Crosses, 256 Silver Stars and 595 Bronze Stars.

According to El Nuevo Día newspaper, May 30, 2004, a total of 756 Puerto Ricans lost their lives in Korea and a total of 3,630 men were wounded, from all four branches of the U.S. Armed Forces. More than half of these were from the 65th Infantry, not including non-Puerto Ricans.

The 65th Infantry returned to Puerto Rico and was deactivated in 1956. However, Major General Juan César Cordero Dávila, Puerto Rico's Adjutant General, 1958–65, persuaded the Department of the Army to transfer the 65th Infantry from the regular Army to the Puerto Rican National Guard.

This was the only unit ever transferred from the active component Army to the Army Guard.

CHAPTER 58

Mass court-martial

After the fighting around Outpost Kelly, Col. Cordero Dávila was relieved of his command by Col. Chester B. DeGavre, a West Point graduate and a "continental" officer from the mainland United States and the officer staff of the 65th was replaced with non-Hispanic officers.

DeGavre ordered that the unit stop calling itself the Borinqueneers, cut their special rations of rice and beans, ordered the men to shave off their mustaches and had one of them wear signs that read "I am a coward".

Throughout October 1952, the 65th's morale declined and casualties around Jackson Heights mounted; by early November a patrol from Company L refused to follow their platoon leader across a river in the Chorwon Valley.

In December 1952, 162 Puerto Ricans of the 65th Infantry were arrested, 95 were court-martialed, and 91 were found guilty and sentenced to prison terms ranging from 1 to 18 years of hard labor. It was the largest mass court-martial of the Korean War.

The Secretary of the Army Robert T. Stevens moved quickly to remit the sentences and granted clemency and pardons to all those involved.

Though the men who were court-martialed were pardoned in 1954, a campaign was later started to obtain a formal exoneration.

An Army report released in 2001 blamed the breakdown of the 65th on the following factors: a shortage of officers and noncommissioned officers, a rotation policy that removed combat-experienced leaders and soldiers, tactics that led to high casualties, an ammunition shortage, communication problems between largely white, English-speaking officers and Spanish-speaking Puerto Rican enlisted men, and declining morale.

The report also found bias in the prosecution of the Puerto Ricans, citing instances of continental soldiers who were not charged after refusing to fight in similar circumstances, before and after Jackson Heights.

Cuban Missile Crisis
Admiral Horacio Rivero Jr.

The Cuban Missile Crisis was a tense confrontation between the Soviet Union and the United States over the Soviet deployment of nuclear missiles in Cuba. On October 22, 1962, Admiral Horacio Rivero Jr. was the commander of the American fleet sent by President John F. Kennedy to set up a quarantine, blockade of the Soviet ships.

On October 28, Soviet Premier Nikita Khrushchev ordered the removal of the Soviet missiles in Cuba, and Kennedy ordered an end of the quarantine of Cuba on November 20, bringing an end to the crisis. Rivero later served as U.S. Ambassador to Spain, 1972–1975.

Vietnam War

During the Vietnam War, an estimated 48,000 Puerto Ricans served in the four branches of the armed forces.

According to a report by the Department of Defense, titled "Number of Puerto Ricans serving in the U.S. Armed Forces during National Emergencies" the total number of Puerto Ricans who died was 455 with 3,775 wounded.

A total of 17 men were listed as Missing in Action, MIA, and of these, PFC Humberto Acosta-Rosario is the only one whose body has never been recovered.

Five Puerto Ricans were awarded the Medal of Honor for actions during the Vietnam War: Staff Sergeant Felix M. Conde-Falcon, Spc4 Héctor Santiago Colón, Captain Eurípides Rubio, PFC Carlos Lozada, and Captain Humbert Roque Versace.

Lance Corporal José L. Rivera, Corporal Miguel Rivera-Sotomayor, and Sergeant Angel Mendez, members of the United States Marine Corps, were awarded the Navy Cross for their heroic actions. Mendez was posthumously awarded the Navy Cross for his actions on March 16, 1967, for saving the life of his platoon commander, Lieutenant Ronald D. Castille, one of the seven justices of the Supreme Court of Pennsylvania. U.S. Senator Charles Schumer has recommended that Mendez' award be upgraded to the Medal of Honor.

Another highly decorated soldier in the Vietnam War was Sergeant First Class Jorge Otero Barreto from the town of Vega Baja, Puerto Rico. He was awarded 38 decorations, among them 2 Silver Star Medals, 5 Bronze Star Medals with "V" for Valor, 4 Army Commendation Medals, 5 Purple Heart Medals and 5 Air Medals.

On September 22, 2015, the Public Broadcasting Service, PBS, documentary. "On Two Fronts: Latinos & Vietnam" by producer Mylène Moreno of Souvenir Pictures, Inc., aired nationwide on PBS and is part of PBS Stories of Service. The documentary focuses on the totality of the Latino experience in Vietnam, not just Puerto Ricans.

Other Puerto Ricans who served in Vietnam and had distinguished military careers include Major General Salvador E. Felices, Rear Admiral Diego E. Hernández, Colonel Héctor Andrés Negroni and Brigadier General Ruben A. Cubero who in 1991 became the first person of Hispanic heritage to be named Dean of Faculty of the United States Air Force Academy.

Two Puerto Ricans who served in Vietnam held positions in the Administration of President George W. Bush. They are Dr. Richard

Carmona, a former Green Beret who was awarded two Purple Hearts and was appointed Surgeon General in March 2002, and Major General William A. Navas Jr., who was awarded the Bronze Star Medal and was named Assistant Secretary of the Navy on June 6, 2001.

Operation El Dorado Canyon

On April 14, 1986, in response to acts of terrorism sponsored by Libyan leader Muammar al-Gaddafi the Berlin disco bombing of April 6—and against the backdrop of heightened tension and clashes between the Libyan and U.S. Navies over Libya's disputed territorial water claims in the Gulf of Sidra, the United States launched a surprise attack on key facilities in Tripoli and other parts of Libya. The attack was code-named Operation El Dorado Canyon.

With the acquiescence of the British government, 24 U.S. Air Force F-111F fighter-bombers took off from U.S. air bases in England. Attacking in the pre-dawn hours of April 15, their main objectives were 22 airfields, terrorist training camps, and other military installations.

Captain Fernando L. Ribas-Dominicci was one of the pilots who participated in the Libyan air raid. His F-111 was shot down over the Gulf of Sidra off the Libyan coast.

Ribas-Dominicci and his weapons systems officer, Captain Paul F. Lorence, were the only U.S. casualties. Al-Qaddafi, who was also personally targeted, escaped harm, but his daughter was killed.

Gulf War and Operation Restore Hope
Captain Manuel Rivera Jr., (USMC)

In 1990, 1,700 Puerto Rican National Guardsmen were among the 20,000 Hispanics deployed to the Persian Gulf in Operations Desert Shield and Desert Storm as part of the Gulf War.

Four Puerto Ricans lost their lives, including Captain Manuel Rivera Jr. of the Marine Corps, a Puerto Rican from the South Bronx, who on January 22, 1991, became the first Marine, and therefore the first Hispanic, to be killed in Operation Desert Shield.

Rivera was killed during a support mission over the Persian Gulf. On January 30, 1991, the U.S. House of Representatives paid tribute to Rivera.

During this era Haydee Javier Kimmich, from Cabo Rojo, Puerto Rico, was the highest-ranking Hispanic female in the Navy when she was promoted to the rank of captain, O-6.

Kimmich was assigned as the Chief of Orthopedics at the Navy Medical Center in Bethesda and reorganized their Reservist Department during Operation Desert Storm. In 1998, she was selected as the woman of the year in Puerto Rico.

Operation Restore Hope was an American military operation with the support of the United Nations that was formed to deliver humanitarian aid and restore order to the African nation of Somalia, then suffering from severe famine, anarchy, and domination by several warlords following the collapse of Siad Barre's Marxist government and the outbreak of the Somali Civil War.

On January 30, 1993, Private First-Class Domingo Arroyo Jr., a Marine from Puerto Rico, became the first of the 44 American soldiers killed during the operation. His patrol was ambushed near Mogadishu, the capital of Somalia, by forces controlled by Somali warlords.

CHAPTER 59

21st century campaigns

September 11 attacks

On September 11, 2001, United Airlines Flight 93 was hijacked by four members of al-Qaeda as part of the September 11 attacks. The hijackers' specific target was the United States Capitol.

Among the pilots available that day of the 113th Wing of the DC Air National Guard were Lieutenant Colonel Marc H. Sasseville and Lieutenant Heather Penney. They were given the mission of finding United Airlines Flight 93 and destroying it.

Since their fighters were not armed with missiles and carrying dummy ammunition from a recent training mission, they might have been required to ram the passenger aircraft.

It was not until hours later that they would learn United 93 had already gone down in a field outside Shanksville, Pennsylvania, killing all 44 people aboard including the four hijackers.

In 2001, Noel Zamot was assigned to the Directorate of Operations, United States Space Command, Paterson Air Force Base in Colorado as Deputy Chief of Operations Integration. According to the United States Air Force, Zamot's mission as Deputy Chief of Operations in the aftermath of the September 11 attacks was to integrate emerging national capabilities into a joint counter-terrorism operation.

He developed concepts for long-term Information Operations and Space Control activities for the US enabling a multi-spectral combat response. He was also involved in the development of the Special Access Program (SAP) systems and in the development of new counter-space capabilities which resulted in a more effective counter-terrorism operation across three combat zones. When he retired from the Air Force, he was commandant of the Test Pilot School at Edwards Air Force Base.

Iraq and Afghanistan
Specialist Lizbeth Robles

In the 21st century, Puerto Ricans have participated in the military campaigns of Afghanistan and Iraq, in what the United States and its allies refer to as the War on Terror. Among those killed in Iraq are the first three Puerto Rican women to die in a foreign combat zone. They are Specialist Frances M. Vega, Specialist Lizbeth Robles, and Specialist Aleina Ramirez Gonzalez.

On November 2, 2003, Specialist Frances M. Vega became the first female Puerto Rican soldier born in the United States to die in a war zone. A ground-to-air missile fired by insurgents in Fallujah hit the Chinook transport helicopter Vega was in; she was one of 16 soldiers who lost their lives in the crash that followed.

On March 1, 2005, Specialist Lizbeth Robles became the first female Puerto Rican soldier born on the island to die in Iraq when her Humvee was involved in an accident.

On July 10, 2007, Captain María Inés Ortiz, who was assigned to a hospital in an area known as the "Green Zone" in Baghdad, Iraq, became the first Puerto Rican nurse to die in combat and the first Army nurse to die in the Iraq War after the area came under a heavy mortar attack.

Specialist Hilda I. Ortiz Clayton, who was of Puerto Rican descent, was a U.S. Army combat photographer killed in 2013 when a mortar exploded during an Afghan training exercise; she was able to photograph the explosion that killed her and four Afghan soldiers.

The 55th Signal Company named their annual competitive award for combat camera work "The Spc. Hilda I. Clayton Best Combat Camera, OMCAM, Competition" in her honor.

Monument of Remembrance
El Monumento de la Recordación

Over 1,225 Puerto Ricans have died while serving the United States. The names of those who perished in combat are inscribed in "El Monumento de la Recordación" Monument of Remembrance, which was unveiled on May 19, 1996, and is situated in front of the Capitol Building in San Juan, Puerto Rico.

On Veterans Day, November 11, 2013, a group representing the Puerto Rican community in Connecticut placed a floral arrangement on the tomb of Augusto Rodrigues, who fought in the American Civil War, recognizing him as Puerto Rico's first known U.S. Armed Forces veteran.

CHAPTER 60

65th Infantry Regiment United States

The 65th Infantry Regiment, nicknamed "The Borinqueneers" during the Korean War for the original Taíno Indian name for Puerto Rico, Borinquen, is a Puerto Rican regiment of the United States Army.

The regiment's motto is Honor et Fidelitas, Latin for Honor and Fidelity. The Army Appropriation Bill created by an act of Congress on 2 March 1899, authorized the creation of the first body of native troops in Puerto Rico. On 30 June 1901, the "Porto Rico Provisional Regiment of Infantry" was organized.

On 1 July 1908, Congress incorporated the regiment into the Regular Army as the Puerto Rico Regiment of Infantry, United States Army.

On 14 May 1917, the regiment was activated, and additional men were assigned, with the unit being sent to serve at Panama.

On 4 June 1920, the regiment was renamed 65th Infantry.[3] During World War II, the regiment saw action throughout Europe, especially France and Germany, participating in Naples-Foggia, Rome-Arno, and Rhin.

Several Purple Hearts were awarded posthumously to members of the 65th Regiment.

The 65th Infantry Regiment participated in World War I, World War II, the Korean War, and the Global War on Terrorism. On 10 June 2014, the 65th Infantry was awarded the Congressional Gold Medal.

Early history

Puerto Ricans have participated in many of the military conflicts in which the United States has been involved.

For example, they participated in the American Revolutionary War, when volunteers from Puerto Rico, Cuba, and Mexico enlisted in the Spanish Army in 1779 and fought under the command of General Bernardo de Gálvez, 1746–1786, and have continued to participate up to the present-day conflicts in Iraq and Afghanistan.

Puerto Rico became a U.S. Territory after the 1898 Treaty of Paris which ended the Spanish American War. The United States appointed a military governor and soon the United States Army established itself in San Juan.

On 2 March 1899, the Army received an assignment of funds and authorization meant to formally organize troops in Puerto Rico.

On 24 March 1899, the General Commander of the Puerto Rico Department, Mayor General Guy V. Henry ordered the creation of the Porto Rico Battalion of Volunteer Infantry.

Formed by four companies named A through D and assigned to San Juan, Mayagüez and Ponce, the unit was activated on 20 May 1899, led by Major Lorenzo Davinson.

Shortly afterwards, each company received additional men for a total of 112. Major Ebon Swift replaced Davison as commander.[8] The formalization of this move was notified in General Order 65, issued by the new General Commander Gen. George Davis.

On 12 February 1900, the Mounted Battalion was organized, and both were later designated Porto Rico Regiment, U.S. Volunteers.

The following year, the units were renamed Porto Rico Provisional Regiment of Infantry. The Band and First Battalion were sent to

Washington on 4 March 1901, to participate in the inauguration of McKinley.

On 1 July 1901, the United States Senate passed a bill which would require a strict mental and physical examination for those who wanted to join the regiment.

It also approved the recruitment of native Puerto Rican civilians to be appointed the grade of second lieutenants for a term of four years if they passed the required tests.

On 23 April 1904, Congress authorized the recruitment of the local population as second lieutenants, leading to the recognition of Jaime Nadal, Henry Rexach, Pedro Parra, Eduardo Iriarte, Teofilo Marxuach, Eugenio María de Hostos, Luis Emmanuelli and Pascual López.

In 1905, one of its battalions was sent to March along with the First a Brigade of the First Division of the Regular Army during Roosevelt's inauguration.

An act of Congress, approved on 27 May 1908, reorganized the regiment as part of the "regular" Army and the "Porto Rico Provisional Regiment of Infantry" was renamed "Porto Rico Regiment of Infantry".

Since the native Puerto Rican officers were Puerto Rican citizens and not citizens of the United States, they were required to undergo a new physical examination to determine their fitness for commissions in the Regular Army and to take an oath of U.S. citizenship with their new officers oath.

By 30 January 1917, the Porto Rico Regiment of Infantry was training in Camp Las Casas, which was in Santurce, a section of San Juan in what is now Residencial Las Casas.

World War I

Different units of the regiment were stationed at other forts throughout the island under the command of William P. Burnham. Lieutenant Teófilo Marxuach, the officer of the day, was stationed at El Morro Castle at San Juan Bay on 21 March 1915.

The Odenwald, built in 1903, not to be confused with the German World War II war ship which carried the same name, was an armed German supply ship which tried to force its way out of the San Juan Bay and deliver supplies to the German submarines waiting in the Atlantic Ocean.

Marxuach gave the order to open fire on the ship from the walls of the fort. Sergeant Encarnacion Correa then manned a machine gun and fired warning shots with little effect.

Marxuach fired a warning shot from a cannon located at the Santa Rosa battery of El Morro fort, in what is the first shot of World War I fired by the regular armed forces of the United States against a ship flying the colors of the Central Powers, forcing the Odenwald to stop and to return to port where its supplies were confiscated.

Casing of the shell fired at the Odenwald

The Odenwald was confiscated by the United States and renamed SS Newport News. It was assigned to the U.S. Shipping Board, where it served until 1924 when it was retired.

Puerto Ricans were unaccustomed to the racial segregation policies of the United States which were also implemented in Puerto Rico, and often refused to designate themselves as "white" or "black".

Puerto Ricans of African descent were assigned to all-black units. In 1916, the Third Battalion and the companies of service and machine-guns were integrated into the regiment.

When the United States declared war against Germany, the regiment was transferred to the regular Army and on 3 May 1917, recruited 1,969 men, considered at that time as war strength.

On 14 May 1917, the regiment was sent to Panama in defense of the Panama Canal Zone.

The regiment returned to Puerto Rico in March 1919 and was renamed "The 65th Infantry Regiment" by the Reorganization Act of 4 June 1920. During this period a young Puerto Rican officer of the

Regular Army, Major Luis R. Esteves, was sent to Camp Las Casas to serve as an instructor in the preparation of Puerto Rican officers. In the future, Esteves would become known as the "Father of the Puerto Rican National Guard".

In 1923, the 65th provided personnel to the newly created 42nd Infantry Regiment.

World War II
Soldiers of the 65th Infantry training in Salinas, Puerto Rico. August 1941

In 1942 the 65th Infantry underwent an extensive training program and in 1943, it was sent to Panama to protect the Pacific and the Atlantic sides of the isthmus.

On 25 November 1943, Colonel Antulio Segarra, succeeded Col. John R. Menclenhall as commander of the 65th Infantry, thus becoming the first Puerto Rican Regular Army officer to command a Regular Army regiment.

In January 1944, the regiment was embarked for Jackson Barracks in New Orleans and later sent to Fort Eustis in Newport News, Virginia in preparation for overseas deployment to North Africa.

They also served in Casablanca after the Naval Battle of Casablanca, where the regiment underwent amphibious training. This enabled the 3rd Battalion to move on to Corsica, where it was attached to the 12th Air Force and tasked with guarding airfields.

Between March and April 1944, the 65th was reassigned to North Africa.

On 3 May 1944, the Third Battalion arrived at Napoles.

The battalion was then moved to Corsica and then to France. Salvador Roig commanded the 65th during this period in Europe, which earned him the Combat Infantryman Badge.

During this time, rumors swirled that the regiment would be sent to live combat, while officers had already been moved to act as observers.

On 22 September 1944, the 65th Infantry landed in France. The regiment was then moved to Peira Cava in the Maritime Alps, where it entered in action on 13 December 1944, the first time a Puerto Rican unit saw action in Europe.

The first offensive attack came the following day in response to enemy fire, with Lieutenant Colonel Juan César Cordero Dávila allowing Capt. Efraín Sánchez Hidalgo and Company L to return fire.

In November 1944, Company C provided security to the headquarters of the Seventh United States Army.[4] The rest of the First Battalion was assigned other tasks, such as defending the Command Center of the Sixth United States Army Group.

The Second and Third Battalions were assigned to defend communications.

In 1948, seven members received the Bronze Star for their service in World War II.

On 13 December 1944, the 65th Infantry, under the command of Lieutenant Colonel Cordero Dávila, relieved the 2nd Battalion of the 442nd Infantry Regiment, a regiment which was made up of Japanese Americans under the command of Col. Virgil R. Miller, a native of San Germán, Puerto Rico and former member of the 65th Infantry Regiment.

In December 1944, the 3rd Battalion faced the German 34th Infantry Division's 107th Grenadier Regiment.

They suffered a total of forty-seven battle casualties. The first two Puerto Ricans to be killed in action from the 65th Infantry were Pvt. Sergio Sánchez-Sánchez and Sgt. Ángel Martínez, from the town of Sabana Grande.

Upon arriving in the freezing and isolated outposts in the Maritime Alps, the unit's morale dropped severely. In an apparent effort to boost the unit's morale, its new commander, West Pointer Colonel George A. Ford, personally led a patrol towards the German lines on 4 January 1945.

Upon reaching the forward German outposts, Colonel Ford was immediately shot and killed. In the firefight that followed, one of the enlisted men already mentioned was killed and several other were wounded, forcing the patrol to abandon the colonel's body.

On 18 March 1945, the regiment was sent to the district of Mannheim, Germany and assigned to military government activities, anti-sabotage, and security missions. In all, the 65th Infantry participated in the campaigns of Rome-Arno, Rhineland, Ardennes-Alsace, and Central Europe.

On 27 October 1945, the regiment sailed from France arriving at Puerto Rico on 9 November 1945.

The 65th Infantry Regiment distinguished itself when the United States conducted a military exercise on the island of Vieques, on the eve of the Korean War.

This exercise was code named "Operation PORTREX," an acronym for "Puerto Rico Exercise." The objective was to see how the combined forces of the Army, Marines, Navy, and Air Force would act as "liberators" of an enemy captured territory, Vieques, against the "aggressors."

The core of the aggressor ground forces were made up of Puerto Rican soldiers, most of whom belonged to the 65th Infantry Regiment.

The liberators consisted of 32,600 combat troops from the 82nd Airborne Division's 504th Airborne Infantry Regiment and the Marine Corps, who received support from the Navy and Air Force.

Despite the large number of troops deployed, the 65th Infantry, the aggressor, was able to halt the offensive forces on the beaches of the island.

Colonel William W. Harris, the commanding officer of the 65th, stated:

"Stopping the assault forces at the water's edge proved that the Puerto Ricans could hold their own against the best-trained soldiers that the United States Army could put into the field."

The successful military maneuvers during PORTREX prompted the Army's leadership to deploy the 65th Infantry to Korea.

Korean War
Company C on patrol

On 27 August 1950, the 65th Infantry, with 3,920 officers and men organized into three infantry battalions, one artillery battalion and a tank company departed from Puerto Rico and arrived in Pusan, South Korea on 23 September 1950.

It was during the long sea voyage that the men nicknamed the 65th Infantry as the "Borinqueneers." "That was the name of the more peaceful of the two original Indian tribes that inhabited the island of Puerto Rico "Borinquen", and many of the men were direct descendants of that industrious race of people."

The men of the 65th, now attached to the Army's 3rd Infantry Division, were among the first infantrymen to meet the enemy on the battlefields of Korea.

After November 1950, they fought daily against units of the Chinese People's Liberation Army after the Chinese entered the war on the North Korean side. The 296th Regiment took its place at Puerto Rico.

In Korea, the regiment covered the retreat of the 1st Marine Division during the Battle of Chosin Reservoir.

One of the hardships suffered by the Puerto Ricans was the lack of warm clothing during the cold, harsh winters. "Born in a semitropical climate- most of them had never seen snow- they had lived and fought through it all without complaint."

The enemy made many attempts to encircle the regiment, but each time they failed because of the many casualties inflicted by the 65th.

Because the 65th held their positions, that enabled the U.S. Marines to withdraw from the Chosin Reservoir in December 1950.

When the Marines were surrounded by the Chinese Communist troops close to the Manchurian border, they were ordered to retreat and work their way back to Hungnam.

The men of the 65th rushed to their defense and were ordered to stay behind and fight the enemy.

As a result, the Marines were able to withdraw to their ships with the 65th holding the rearguard. The 65th, attached to the 1st Marine Division, was awarded the Navy Unit Commendation for their defense and were among the last units to embark from Hungnam.

Among the battles and operations in which the 65th participated was Operation Killer in January 1951, becoming the first regiment to cross the Han River in South Korea during the operation.

In April 1951, the regiment participated in the Uijonbu Corridor drives and in June 1951, the 65th was the third regiment to cross the Han Ton River.

The 65th took and held Chorwon and they were also instrumental in breaking the Iron Triangle of Hill 717 in July 1951.

In November 1951, the regiment fought off an attack by two regimental size enemy units.

Colonel Juan César Cordero Dávila of the 296th Regiment requested a transfer to active service in Korea.

In December 1951, Chief of Staff J. Lawton Collins visited Puerto Rico and granted the request, reassigning him to the 65th, replacing him with Lt. Col. Sepúlveda.

Col. Cordero was formally named commander of the 65th Infantry on 8 February 1952, thus becoming one of the highest-ranking ethnic officers in the Army.

Brigadier William Warner Harris, USMA 1930, published a book that captured the distinguished history of the 65th century while under his command.

When asked if the Puerto Ricans would fight when the time came, then Colonel William Warner Harris' answer was just as direct: "My Puerto Ricans will fight anyone, anywhere."

CHAPTER 61

Battles of Outpost Kelly and Jackson Heights

On 3 July 1952, the regiment defended the main line of resistance, MLR, for 47 days and saw action at Cognac, King, and Queen with successful attacks on Chinese positions.

In September 1952, the 65th Infantry defended a hill known as Outpost Kelly. Chinese Communist forces overran the hill in what became known as the Battle of Outpost Kelly. On two occasions, the 65th Regiment was overwhelmed by Chinese artillery and driven off.

In October 1952, the regiment also saw action in the Chorwon Sector and on Iron Horse, Hill 391, whose lower part was called "Jackson Heights" in honor of Capt. George Jackson.

Company G of the 65th fought a desperate battle to hold on to Hill 391. After enduring days of artillery bombardment with limited artillery support of their own, Company G withdrew to avoid being overrun by a numerically superior foe.

In June 1953, the 2nd Battalion conducted a series of successful raids about two and a half miles southeast of Jackson Heights and in November the regiment successfully counter-attacked enemy units in the Numsong Valley and held their positions until the armistice was reached.

Many non-Puerto Rican Hispanics served in the 65th Infantry during the war. Among those who distinguished themselves in combat and who served in the conflict as a member of the 65th Infantry was a young first lieutenant of Mexican American descent whose name is Richard Edward Cavazos.

Cavazos entered the military in Texas and served as company commander of Company E of the 2d Battalion. Cavazos, who in 1982, became the first Hispanic to become a four-star general in the United States Army, was the recipient of the Distinguished Service Cross, the Silver Star Medal, and the Bronze Star Medal.

Mass court martial

Soldiers of the 65th, North of the Han River, Korea, June 1951.

Col. Cordero Dávila was relieved of his command by Col. Chester B. DeGavre, a West Point graduate and a "Continental," an officer from the mainland United States, and the officer staff of the 65th was replaced with non-Hispanic officers.

DeGavre, upset over the fact that "G" company did not hold on to Hill 391, ordered that the unit stop calling itself the "Borinqueneers," cut their special rations of rice and beans, ordered the men to shave off their mustaches, and had one of them wear a sign that read: "I am a coward."

The language barrier, an NCO shortage, and poor leadership were factors that influenced some of the men of Company L in their refusal to continue to fight.

One hundred and sixty-two Puerto Ricans of the 65th Infantry were arrested. Between 23 November, 26 December 1952, ninety-five soldiers were tried by General Court-Martial in fifteen separate trials. Ninety-one were found guilty and sentenced to prison terms ranging from one to 18 years of hard labor.

It was the largest mass court-martial of the Korean War. According to cultural historian Silvia Álvarez Curbelo, the government of Puerto Rico, caught in the middle of a potentially damaging affair that could jeopardize its political agenda, kept silent for nearly two months.

Finally, the incidents were made known by a local newspaper alerted by letters written by the imprisoned soldiers to their families. Secret negotiations between the U.S. and Puerto Rican governments took place and the Secretary of the Army Robert T. Stevens moved quickly to remit the sentences and grant clemency and pardons to all those involved.

The breakdown of the 65th resulted from several factors: a shortage of officers and non-commissioned officers, a rotation policy that removed combat-experienced leaders and soldiers, tactical doctrine that led to high casualties, a shortage of artillery ammunition, communication problems between largely white, English-speaking officers and Spanish-speaking Puerto Rican enlisted men, and declining morale.

The report also found bias in the prosecution of the Puerto Ricans, citing instances of Continental soldiers who were not charged after refusing to fight in similar circumstances, before and after Jackson Heights.

Though the men who were court martialed were pardoned, a campaign for a formal exoneration was launched.

CHAPTER 62

Awards in the Korean War

Master Sergeant Juan E. Negrón was awarded the Distinguished Service Cross for his courageous actions while serving as a member of Company L, 65th Infantry Regiment, 3d Infantry Division during combat operations against an armed enemy in Kalma-Eri, Korea 28 April 1951. His award was upgraded to the Medal of Honor on 18 March 2014.

Master Sergeant Juan E Negron

For service as set forth in the following citation: The Medal of Honor is posthumously presented to Juan E. Negrón, RA10406243, Master Sergeant, U.S. Army, for extraordinary heroism in connection with military operations against an armed enemy of the United Nations while serving with the 65th Infantry Regiment, 3d Infantry Division.

Master Sergeant Negrón distinguished himself by extraordinary heroism in action against enemy aggressor forces in the vicinity of Kalma-Eri, Korea, on 28 April 1951.

On that date, Sergeant Negrón took up the most vulnerable position on his company's exposed right flank after an enemy force had overrun a section of the line.

When notified that elements of the company were withdrawing, Sergeant Negrón refused to leave his exposed position, but delivered withering fire at hostile troops who had broken through a roadblock.

When the hostile troops approached his position, Sergeant Negrón accurately hurled hand grenades at short range, halting their attack. Sergeant Negrón held the position throughout the night, while an allied counterattack was organized and launched.

After the enemy had been repulsed, fifteen enemy dead were found only a few feet from Sergeant Negron's position. The extraordinary heroism exhibited by Sergeant Negrón on this occasion reflects great credit on himself and is in keeping with the finest traditions of the military service.

A total of 61,000 Puerto Ricans served in the military during the Korean War. And around 90% of the Puerto Ricans that saw action in Korea were volunteers.

The 65th Infantry was awarded battle participation credits for the following nine campaigns: UN Defense-1950, UN Offense-1950, CCF Intervention-1950, First UN Counterattack Offensive-1951, UN and CCF Spring Offensive-1951, UN Summer-Fall Offensive-1951, 2nd Korean Winter 1951–52, Korean Summer-Fall-1952 and 3rd Korean Winter-1952-53.

They are credited with the last battalion-sized bayonet charge in U.S. Army history.

Individual awards in the Korean War

Award	Name Total
Medal of Honor	1
Army distinguished service cross medal.jpg	
Distinguished Service Cross	10
Silver Star medal.png	
Silver Star	256
Bronze Star medal	
Bronze Star	606

Purple Heart Medal.
Purple Heart   2,771

Ten Distinguished Service Crosses, 256 Silver Stars and 606 Bronze Stars for valor were awarded to the men of the 65th Infantry. Of the ten Distinguished Service Crosses that were awarded to the members of the 65th Infantry, five were awarded to Puerto Ricans:

Sergeant First Class Modesto Cartagena
Private Badel Hernández Guzmán
Master Sergeant Juan E. Negrón, upgraded to the Medal of Honor
Corporal Fabián Nieves Laguer
Master Sergeant Belisario Noriega

According to El Nuevo Día newspaper, 30 May 2004, a total of 756 Puerto Ricans were killed in Korea, from all four branches of the U.S. armed forces.

However, according to "All POW-MIA Korean War Casualties", the total number of Puerto Rican casualties in the Korean War was 732. However, this total may vary slightly since some non-Puerto Ricans such as Captain James W. Conner were mistakenly included.

Out of the 700 plus casualties suffered in the war a total of 121 men were listed as missing in action.

The Battle of Outpost Kelly accounted for 73 of the men missing in action from the total of 121.

Out of the 73 MIAs suffered by the regiment in September 1952, 50 of them occurred on the same day, 18 September. For a list of names of those who were declared MIA.

According to the TAGOKOR Korean War Casualty File and the American Battle Commission site the members of the 65th who fought in Korea were awarded a total of 2,771 Purple Heart Medals.

On 12 February 1951, General Douglas MacArthur, wrote in Tokyo:

The Puerto Ricans forming the ranks of the gallant 65th Infantry give daily proof on the battlefields of Korea of their courage, determination and resolute will to victory, their invincible loyalty to the United States and their fervent devotion to those immutable principles of human relations which the Americans of the Continent and of Puerto Rico have in common.

They are writing a brilliant record of heroism in battle, and I am indeed proud to have them under my command. I wish that we could count on many more like them.

General Richard E. Cavazos, the first Mexican American to reach the rank of brigadier general in the U.S. Army

The 65th Infantry was relieved from assignment to the 3d Infantry Division on 3 November 1954, and, returning to Puerto Rico, it was assigned on 2 December 1954, to the 23rd Infantry Division, which encompassed geographically separated units in the Caribbean region.

On 10 April 1956, it was inactivated at Losey Field, Puerto Rico, and relieved from assignment to the 23d, which itself was inactivated.

Sergeant Modesto Cartagena, the most decorated Hispanic U.S. soldier in the Korean War.

On 6 February 1959, the regiment was deactivated from the Regular Army, but the Puerto Rican Army National Guard soon adopted "65" as the identifying number for their existing 296th Regimental Combat Team at Losey Field, mainly composed of reserve component personnel.

On 15 February 1959, it was organized to consist of the 1st Battle Group, 65th Infantry, an element of the 92nd Infantry Brigade.

On 21 February 1960, commemorated as National Guard Day, the 65th Infantry Regiment was formally transferred from the Regular Army to the PRNG, in an activity where General Cesár Cordero handed the units colors to Col. Rafael Rodríguez.

That same year, Company B of the 65th Regiment created Employer's Day, Día del Patrono in Spanish, where the employers of the volunteers that serve in the PRNG are instructed about the job that their employees do with the entity and participate in training of their own.

The idea behind the initiative was facilitating the processing of the request of leave-of-absence to train for two weeks during the summer. On 1 May 1964, it was reorganized to consist of the 1st Battalion, 65th Infantry, and remained assigned to the 92nd.

It was reorganized again on 1 April 1971, to consist of the 1st Battalion and the separate Company E. This was followed by another reorganization on 1 September 1978, to consist of the 1st and 2nd Battalions within the 92nd, as well as the separate Company E. Less than two years later another reorganization on 29 February 1980, eliminated the separate Company E while retaining the 1st and 2nd Battalions.

On 27 October 1987, the regiment was withdrawn from CARS and reorganized under the United States Army Regimental System with headquarters at Cayey.

It was reorganized on 1 September 1992, to consist of the 1st Battalion, 65th Infantry, and remained assigned to the 92nd Infantry Brigade.

On 14 February 2003, it was ordered into active federal service at home stations and released on 12 February 2005, reverting to territorial control.

On 1 October of that year, it was reorganized as the 65th Infantry Regiment in which only the 1st Battalion was active.

The separate Company E was a Ranger unit given federal recognition effective 1 April 1971, and had a total authorized strength of 198 personnel.

It was added to the PR ARNG on that date while the 755th Transportation Company, Medium Truck, Cargo, was deleted. Co E, Ranger, 65th Infantry relocated from Vega Baja to San Juan on 2 February 1976, and was inactivated as federal recognition was withdrawn effective 29 February 1980.

This resulted in the allocation of an ARNG ranger company being transferred from the PR ARNG to the Texas ARNG, in which Company G, Ranger, 143rd Infantry was activated in Houston from elements of the 2d Battalion, Airborne, 143rd Infantry, 36th Airborne Brigade, which was being inactivated effective 1 April 1980.

Twenty-first century

The 65th Infantry Regiment's 1st Battalion, along with its sister battalion, the 1–296th Infantry, was transferred to the 92nd Infantry Brigade, PRARNG, now the 92nd Maneuver Enhancement Brigade.

Both battalions have served in what the United States Department of Defense calls the Global War on Terrorism, as well as the Iraq War.

In 2009, Company C, 1st Battalion, 65th Infantry Regiment was deployed to the Horn of Africa and stationed at Camp Lemonnier in Djibouti, after completing a 14-month deployment at Guantanamo Bay, Cuba.

Company C carried the crew-served weapons to protect the camp. It also operated the entry control checkpoints, protected U.S. and allied ships at the massive Djibouti Port and guarded the U.S. Embassy there.

By mid-2009, the rest of the battalion deployed there in case a larger combat maneuver element was needed to operate from the base. The area is the most unstable part of Africa, and the Somali border is less than 10 miles from Camp Lemonnier.

CHAPTER 63

Legacy

Amonument dedicated to the 65th Infantry Regiment in Río Piedras, Puerto Rico

During the Korean War, the Borinqueneers were awarded 10 Distinguished Service Crosses, Juan Negrons was upgraded to the Medal of Honor, 256 Silver Stars, 606 Bronze Stars, and 2,771 Purple Hearts.

Puerto Rico honored the unit by naming one of its principal avenues "Avenida 65 de Infantería" in San Juan. The names of those killed in combat are inscribed in "El Monumento de la Recordación", Monument of Remembrance, which was unveiled on 19 May 1996 and is situated in front of the Capitol Building in San Juan, Puerto Rico.

In November 1999, Governor Pedro Rosselló, along with the Senate of Puerto Rico, chartered the 65th Infantry Honor Task Force and appointed Anthony Mele as chairman to work with Major General Nels Running, director, Committee of the 50th Anniversary of the Korean War to commemorate the 65th Infantry Regiment.

The 65th Infantry Honor Task Force is a coalition of individuals, veterans organizations, and groups dedicated to advocate and preserve the legacy of the 65th Infantry Regiment.

The group organized tree planting and plaque commemoration ceremonies around the US, to include Arlington National Cemetery in

Virginia; Fort San Felipe del Morro in San Juan, Puerto Rico; and Fort Logan National Cemetery in Denver.

On 20 May 2001, the government of Puerto Rico unveiled a monument honoring the 65th Infantry Regiment.

The monument was made by artist Sonny Rodríguez and is called "Mission Accomplished".

It contains a statue of a soldier wearing a poncho with his rifle in one hand and the regiment's flag in the other hand.

On 7 June 2007, PBS aired The Borinqueneers, a documentary about the 65th Infantry written and directed by Noemí Figueroa Soulet with Raquel Ortiz as co-director. The narrators were Héctor Elizondo in English and David Ortiz-Anglero, in Spanish.

On 30 November 2012, an entire stretch of Southern Boulevard in the South Bronx, New York was named La 65 de Infantería Boulevard.

On 1 October 2013, the 65th Infantry Honor Task Force organized veterans from the 65th and their families to attend a salute to the regiment by the 3rd U.S. Infantry "The Old Guard" at Fort Myer, Virginia, a tour of the Tomb of the Unknown Soldiers, and wreath laying ceremony at the Korean War Veterans Memorial in Washington, D.C. 22–23 March 2014, the 65th Infantry Honor Task Force organized the salute of the first Medal of Honor awarded to a Borinqueneer; MSG Juan E. Negron in New York with Iris Negron, daughter of MSG Negron, and BG Jose Burgos.

In attendance were New York State Senators William E. Larkin, a Korean War combat veteran, and David Carlucci who presented a proclamation from the New York State Senate.

In 2014 the National Puerto Rican Day Parade, which is attended by nearly two million people and broadcast live on Fox TV, was dedicated to the Borinqueneers.

On May 25, 2018, the city of the city of Springfield, Massachusetts unveiled "65th Infantry Way".

On December 13, 2019, US President Donald Trump signed into law the H.R.2325 legislation to designate the facility of the United States

Postal Service located at 100 Calle Alondra in Río Piedras, Puerto Rico, as the "65th Infantry Regiment Post Office Building".

On January 27, 2020, an entry gate Fort Buchanan in Puerto Rico was officially renamed "The Borinqueneers Gate" in honor the 65th Infantry Regiment.

In early 2021, a law was signed to make April 13 National Day of Borinqueneers so that veterans could commemorate the service of Borinqueneers. April 13 was chosen because it was the day when members of the unit received a Congressional Gold Medal in 2016.

There is a monument to the Borinqueneers in Korea. The 65th Infantry Regiment Association, led by Victor Labarca, works with all matters related to the 65th Infantry Regiment and its service members.

CHAPTER 64

Congressional Gold Medal

Borinqueneers Congressional Gold Medal

Design of the Congressional Gold Medal which was awarded to the Borinqueneers of the 65th Infantry Regiment.

A Congressional Gold Medal is an award bestowed by the United States Congress and is, along with the Presidential Medal of Freedom, the highest civilian award in the United States.

It is awarded to persons "who have performed an achievement that has an impact on American history and culture that is likely to be recognized as a major achievement in the recipient's field long after the achievement."

While a civilian award, generally recognizing single individuals politicians, scientists, actors, military leaders, civilian heroes, and others, or small groups, people who took a stand for civil rights and others, Congressional Gold Medals have also been awarded to a few military units, such as the Native American code talkers, and the Japanese American 100th Infantry Battalion and 442nd Infantry Regiment, the Tuskegee Airmen, and others.

In 2013, S. 1726, a bill to confer the Congressional Gold Medal on the 65th Infantry Regiment, was introduced in Congress.

It was signed by President Barack Obama at a ceremony on 10 June 2014, becoming Public Law 113–120.

A decision on the design for the medal was awarded in 2015, after the Citizens Coinage Advisory Committee agreed on a choice from submitted designs on 16 June 2015.

The 65th Infantry Borinqueneers Congressional Gold Medal has, for the obverse, a design depicting a close-up portrait of a unit staff sergeant, with three soldiers traversing rocky ground in the background.

The reverse features an historic sentry box in Old San Juan, Puerto Rico, an olive branch, the 65th Infantry insignia patch and unit's motto, HONOR ET FIDELITAS, Honor and Fidelity, and a short list showing "1899–1956" "World War I" "World War II" "Korean War".

On 13 April 2016, leaders of the United States House and Senate officially awarded the Congressional Gold Medal to the 65th Infantry Regiment. Beginning in 2021, National Borinqueneers Day is celebrated on April 13.

CHAPTER 65

The Korean War the first time Puerto Rican troops were thrown in

No conflict has been as impactful and transformative for Puerto Rico and Puerto Ricans as the Korean War.

In slightly over three years of fighting some 61,000 Puerto Ricans served in the U.S. Armed Forces.

The Puerto Rican involvement in the Korean War was as large as in World War II, a war of a global scale, and larger than in Vietnam, the longest American conflict to that point.

The Korean War was also the first time Puerto Rican troops were thrown into combat in large numbers, as Puerto Rican units, and for a prolonged period since they started serving in the Unites States Armed Forces in 1899.

Most of the Puerto Ricans who served in this war were members of the 65th United States Army Infantry Regiment.

During the war, this regiment, known as "el sesenta y cinco", and its men, the Borinqueneers, became a national icon representing the hopes of a people willing to sacrifice their youth for a better future, acceptance and respectability, equality, a path towards decolonization, and a democracy that had and has proven elusive to them.

The significance of the Puerto Rican participation in the Forgotten War had been lost and it was not until recently that these histories started to be uncovered, eventually leading to Congress awarding the Congressional Gold Medal to the 65th in recognition of their service.

The award also recognizes that when the 65th fought under the flags of Puerto Rico, the United States, and the United Nations, they did so carry an undue burden.

Borinqueneers Congressional Gold Medal

The "Borinqueneers Congressional Gold Medal" is a Congressional Gold Medal awarded to Puerto Rico's 65th Infantry Regiment by President Barack Obama, at an official ceremony on June 10, 2014. On May 19, 2014, the United States House of Representatives passed the Bill, known as HR 1726 and three days later May 22, 2014, the Senate approved Bill S. 1174.

With the approval of both houses, the president signed the legislation which awarded the Congressional Gold Medal to the 65th Infantry, the first segregated Hispanic military unit, and the first unit of the Korean War, to receive such distinction.

65th Infantry Regiment

The 65th Infantry Regiment, nicknamed "The Borinqueneers" from the original Taíno name of the island, Borinquen, was a segregated Puerto Rican regiment of the United States Army.

The 65th Infantry Regiment participated in World War I, World War II and the Korean War. Congressional Gold Medal

A Congressional Gold Medal is an award bestowed by the United States Congress and is, along with the Presidential Medal of Freedom, the highest civilian award in the United States.

It is awarded to persons "who have performed an achievement that has an impact on American history and culture that is likely to be recognized as a major achievement in the recipient's field long after the achievement."

As of 2013, four military units had been awarded the Congressional Gold Medal. These were the Navaho Wind Talkers, Native American Marines whose primary job was the transmission of secret tactical messages with the use of their Native language; the Nisei Soldiers - Japanese American intelligence soldiers during WWII in the Pacific, Africa, Italy and France; the Tuskegee Airmen, the first African American military aviators; and the Montford Point Marines, the first African Americans to break the race barrier in the Marines.

In addition, the Women's Air Service Pilots (WASP) received the Congressional Gold Medal.

Congressional Gold Medal initiative

The bill that would confer the Congressional Gold Medal on the 65th Infantry Regiment was introduced in both the United States House of Representatives and in the United States Senate.

For the bill to become law and the medal to be conferred, one of those bills would have to pass in both chambers and be signed by the President of the United States.

H.R. 1726 was introduced into the House of Representatives on April 25, 2013, by Representative Bill Posey of Florida and Pedro Pierluisi, Puerto Rico's Resident Commissioner to the U.S. Congress.

S. 1174 was introduced into the Senate on June 18, 2013, by Senator Richard Blumenthal of Connecticut.[9] The two bills, H.R. 1726, and S. 1174, were formally recognized as "identical bills" by the Congressional Research Service.

This meant that they were "word-for-word identical."

Section two of the bill reads as follows

The Speaker of the House of Representatives and the President pro tempore of the Senate shall make appropriate arrangements for the award, on behalf of the Congress, of a single gold medal of appropriate design in honor of the 65th Infantry Regiment, known as the Borinqueneers, in recognition of its pioneering military service, devotion to duty, and many acts of valor in the face of adversity.

Borinqueneers CGM Alliance, which promoted the Congressional Gold Medal for the 65th Infantry

Advocates garnered over 25 regional proclamations and resolutions signed by governors, mayors, county commissioners and state senators/representatives throughout the U.S., all urging the U.S. Congress to award the Congressional Gold Medal to the 65th Infantry. There are also 10 memorials and monuments honoring the 65th Infantry around the nation.

On 14 August 2013, the Vietnam Veterans of America, a congressional-chartered veterans service organization, issued a national resolution in favor of the Congressional Gold Medal for the 65th Infantry Regiment.

Also in August 2013, the Hispanic American Veterans of Connecticut announced their support of the CGM initiative.

Other national organizations supporting the Congressional Gold Medal initiative include the League of United Latin American Citizens (LULAC), Military Order of the Purple Heart (MOPH), American GI Forum (AGIF), and National Puerto Rican Coalition (NPRC).

Individuals and organizations around the U.S. are currently advocated for the passage of both 65th Infantry CGM bills.

They urged their federal elected officials to join on as co-sponsors of HR 1726 in the House, and S 1174 in the Senate.

The Borinqueneers Congressional Gold Medal Alliance, officially sponsored by the You Are Strong! Center on Veterans Health and Human Services was the leading organization dedicated to the effort.

Congressional Gold Medal legislation

The Bill, known as HR 1726, passed favorably in the House on May 19, 2014. Three days later on May 22, 2014, the Senate approved Bill S. 1174.

The Borinqueneers CGM Bill went to President Barack Obama, who signed the legislation, since then known as Public Law 113-120, at an official ceremony on June 10, 2014. The 65th Infantry is the first Hispanic military unit, and the first unit of the Korean War, to be awarded the Congressional Gold Medal.

Congressional Gold Medal design

A decision on designs for a congressional gold medal being awarded in 2015 to the Borinqueneers of the 65th Infantry Regiment was selected by the Citizens Coinage Advisory Committee on June 16, 2015.

For the 65th Infantry Borinqueneers congressional gold medal, the CCAC recommended for the obverse a design depicting a close-up portrait of a unit staff sergeant, with three soldiers traversing rocky ground in the background.

The recommended reverse features an historic sentry box in Old San Juan, Puerto Rico, an olive branch, the 65th Infantry insignia patch and unit's motto, HONOR ET FIDELITAS (Honor and Fidelity).

However, the gold medal design process and candidate design did not achieve unanimous support among various members of the Borinqueneers community. Some Borinqueneers advocates were not satisfied with the lack of fairness, inclusion, and transparency of the medal design process itself.

In August 2015, the Borinqueneers CGM design was finally approved by the Secretary of the Treasury.

On April 13, 2016, leaders of the United States House and Senate awarded the Congressional Gold Medal to the 65th Infantry Regiment.

REFERENCES

"Special Designation Listing". United States Army Center of Military History. 21 April 2010. Archived from the original on 9 June 2010. Retrieved 14 July 2010.

NBC News, "A Soldier's Mission to Honor Segregated 65th Regiment 'Borinqueneers'", retrieved August 7, 2014

"Congressional Research Service, Congressional Gold Medals, 1776-2012 CRS Report RL30076". senate.gov. Retrieved 2012-09-09.

"Congressional Gold Medals go to Nisei veterans"; By Carlos Alcalá; Published: Sunday, May. 27, 2012 Archived July 14, 2014, at the Wayback Machine

The White House; Honoring our Serviceman; March 29, 2007

"Most Popular E-mail Newsletter". USA Today. 28 June 2012.

Contact Senators and Congressmen to Adopt "Borinqueneers Congressional Gold Medal Bill" H.R. 1726; Tucson Citizen; 5/10/2013; by Dee Dee Garcia Blasé[permanent dead link] Retrieved 13 August 2013.

The Borinqueneers: Award Them the Gold; The Daily Kos; 5/27/2013; by Denise Oliver Velez, Retrieved 13 August 2013

"S. 1174 - Summary". United States Congress. 18 June 2013. Retrieved 19 May 2014.

"H.R. 1726 - Related Bills". United States Congress. Retrieved 19 May 2014.

"Legislative Glossary". United States Congress. Retrieved 19 May 2014.

Bill Text: H.R.1726, Library of Congress

Bill Summary Status: S.1174, Library of Congress

Puerto Rico Herald - Puerto Rico Perfil: El Regimiento del 65 de Infantería en Corea Archived September 24, 2012, at the Wayback Machine, Retrieved 8 September 2007

Push to Honor Puerto Rican Regiment Gains Momentum, New Britain Herald;by Johnny J. Burnham; 8/13/2013. Retrieved 18 August 2013.

Recognize the Borinqueneers Ahora!; Fox News Latino; 8/26/13; by Larry Brystran. Retrieved 26 August 2013.

Former Bridgeport Man a Driving Force Behind Borinqueneers Effort; Connecticut Latino News; 7/1/2013; by Barbara Thomas Archived 2013-10-29 at the Wayback Machine Retrieved 13 August 2013.

Borinqueneers Congressional Gold Medal Alliance

Obama honors Puerto Rican Infantry Regiment with Congressional Gold Medal, Washington Post, June 10, 2014.

Dan Friedman, "Puerto Rico's Borinqueneers recognized with Congressional Gold Medal," New York Daily News, June 11, 2014.

Obama awards Borinqueneers Congressional Medal of Honor, NBC News, June 10, 2014.

Richard Payerchin, "President Obama to honor Army's Puerto Rican regiment the Borinqueneers," The Morning Journal, June 9, 2014.

Maricarmen Agosto, "La heroica y olvidada historia de los Borinqueneers," El Nuevo Herald, Nov. 24, 2014.

"CCAC reviews designs for Borinqueneers' congressional gold medal".

"Desacuerdo entre Borinqueneers por diseño de medalla de oro | la Prensa". Archived from the original on 2016-03-07. Retrieved 2016-03-03.

"In CT It's a Go for Borinqueneers, Nationally Left Out of Medal Design | ctlatinonews.com". Archived from the original on 2016-03-09. Retrieved 2016-03-03.

Archived at Ghostarchive and the Wayback Machine: Borinqueneers Dissatisfied with Congressional Gold Medal Design-Kissimmee, FL June 19, 2015. YouTube.

"Design for Borinqueneers' Congressional Gold Medal has been approved".

Congress honors Army's Borinqueneers with gold medal

ABOUT THE AUTHOR

Norma Iris Pagan Morales was born in Ponce, Puerto Rico. Her parents, Juan Jose Pagan Rodriguez, and Digna Morales Figueroa, now deceased, always helped her with her projects as a writer and teaching career.

Norma had three siblings, Adelin Milagros Pagan Morales, Juan Jose Pagan Morales, and Julio Manuel Pagan Morales. Julio Manuel Pagan Morales died on September 19, 1998. He was also known for his writing / composer skills.

On February 17, 2023, Adelin Milagros Pagan Morales, her sister, died in the City of New York

Norma did all her academic studies in New York City, Puerto Rico, and Canada. She worked in the City of New York Police Department where she oversaw the full investigation of every new civilian and uniform member of the department.

As an Educator, she worked in New York City Bd. of Education, in Puerto Rico Bd. of Education as an English teacher. She also worked for the Puerto Rico Army National as an English Teacher.

She has teaching certifications for English as a Second Language and Teaching English as a Foreign Language. She also has teaching licenses to teach the following:

1. English Literature
2. Spanish Literature
3. Communication Skills in both English and Spanish
4. Office Procedures= These classes consisted of basic filing to writing memorandums and full company or organization reports.
5. Computers - Certified to teach Long Distance Learning

She has published 18 books: Proud of My Puerto Rican Bequest, Porque Soy Boricua? Poemas del Alma, Art in Written Form, A Baffling Short Stories Collection, On Job in the Big Apple, Nature's Rage in the Caribbean, You are the One, The Unfaithful, Poemas Tiernos, Two Strangers, Puerto Rican Soldiers Serving with Pride, Two Strangers to name a few...

www.ingramcontent.com/pod-product-compliance
Lightning Source LLC
Chambersburg PA
CBHW021620120626
46545CB00001B/317

* 9 7 8 1 9 5 9 8 9 5 9 6 1 *